Word-Processing Technology in Japan

Word-Processing Technology in Japan

Kanji and the Keyboard

Nanette Gottlieb

CURZON

First Published in 2000
by Curzon Press
Richmond, Surrey
http://www.curzonpress.co.uk

Typeset in Garamond by LaserScript Ltd, Mitcham, Surrey
Printed and bound in Great Britain by
TJ International, Padstow, Cornwall

British Library Cataloguing in Publication Data
A catalogue record of this book is available from the British Library

Library of Congress Cataloguing in Publication Data
A catalogue record for this book has been requested

ISBN 0–7007–1222–4

For my family

Contents

Acknowledgments

Many people have given me valuable help in the preparation of this book. My sincere thanks are due to the Australian Research Council which provided the funding for the research. Research assistants Donna Weeks and Gretchen Evans did much of the legwork in finding and summarising sources, compiling bibliographies and offering perceptive comments. I thank Professor Mizutani Osamu of the National Language Research Institute in Tokyo for the use of the Institute library; Professors Ogino Tsunao and Yamada Hisao for generously providing details of their research; Mr Yasunaga Minoru of the Japanese Language Section of Japan's Education Ministry for discussions on the attitude of the National Language Council to the word processor issue; and colleagues for their comments on the various drafts of sections of the work presented at conferences and seminars. And as always, thanks to Hans, Susan and Greg for their endless support and patience during the writing of this book.

Part of the research for this book has appeared in earlier form in the *Asian Studies Review*, *Japan Forum*, *Japanese Studies* and the *South Pacific Journal of Psychology* and is used here by kind permission of the editors.

Introduction

One of the most important developments in the history of Japan's writing system has been the invention of character-capable word processing technology which has enabled characters to be handled electronically, thereby solving what had seemed an intractable problem for machine production of documents. The nature of the Japanese script, in particular the use of a large set of kanji (Chinese characters), for a long time worked against office automation, to the extent that Japan did not experience a successful typewriter era as did the west. With the unveiling of the first word processor in 1978 came a sense of liberation from the constraints imposed by the writing system in company offices and, a few years later, in homes and universities as well. So great was the change that one commentator hailed this technology as worthy of an Order of Cultural Merit.

Within Japan itself, the rapid spread of this technology since the early 1980s is perceived to be bringing about changes in orthographic practice which are likely to have implications for national script policy as Japan moves into the next century. This book, which seeks to understand the social significance of the impact of the technology for the lives and writing habits of its users, examines the changing relationship between writer and text and illuminates the engagement between an advanced technology and an ancient orthography. If 'cultural forms (are) the critical sites of struggle upon which various social groups attempt to define the boundaries of social meaning' (Lee, 1993: 48), then word processing technology in Japan represents one such cultural site of dispute. It is the central focus of a struggle to redefine the boundaries of social and orthographic practice as writing begins to change from the manifestation of a paper-based culture to that of a screen-based environment. On the global scene, this technology has enabled Japan to construct a substantial and rapidly increasing presence on the Internet, despite continuing difficulties with international standards of character coding. It has knocked away the underpinning for the argument that Japan would have to romanise in order to achieve a successful computer age, privileging the maintenance of domestic infrastructure and affective attachment to script over considerations of international convenience.

The now largely outdated technological determinist viewpoint posits that changes in technology are the most important cause of social change, with the technologies themselves and their developers seen as somehow unaffected by, or in some sense isolated from, economic or political imperatives of the societies in which they function. Technology is seen as somehow bringing about change within a society without itself being shaped by that society in the first place. Wajcman (1994: 4), for example, points out what seems only common sense, that technological development is an evolutionary process arising out of incremental change in existing technology, with even those advances hailed as revolutionary having been through a long process of this kind: "Existing technology is thus an important precondition of new technology. But it is not the only force shaping new technology. Technological systems are oriented to a goal and that goal is normally about reducing costs and increasing revenues." When a technology is developed to address perceived inefficiencies in a system, she continues, inefficient usually means uneconomical; there is thus an indivisible relationship between technology and economics.

This is certainly true in the case of word processing technology in Japan, which of course was developed in a business context in order to address the perceived inefficiencies of the Japanese typewriter and of the overall deficiencies in office sector productivity as compared to advances in factory productivity due to automation. As we shall see in the following chapters, the nature of the Japanese script, and specifically of the size of the character set, made of the Japanese typewriter a bulky, cumbersome and slow machine which required specialist training to operate and was not readily portable. While typewriters were at different stages developed which used only the hiragana and/or katakana phonetic scripts, the resultant text did not satisfy its readers because that was not the way Japanese was really written, and such machines tended to be used only for specific purposes such as billing rather than for more widely applicable tasks. Changes in the printing industry and in newspaper production also added pressure to the need to find a way of handling characters efficiently. In addition to the focus on the actual mechanical aspects of document production, a further consideration was that word processing would bring to an end the office dependency on specialist typists, enabling increased productivity on the part of ordinary office workers (who were not usually trained typists) and lower management. Typist wages made up only a small part of the overall office wage bill; the aim was to introduce a technology that a much wider spectrum of staff could operate. Economic considerations were therefore most certainly involved in the development of character-capable word processing, both from the point of view of the companies which would form its main market in the beginning and that of the producer companies who saw that market waiting. It was clear that romanisation, proposed by some as the only way out of the office automation difficulty, was never going to be an acceptable solution for Japan, given the overall cost of changing the existing script-oriented infrastructure it would have involved, not to mention the strength of affective attachments to the existing orthography.

When the technology began its rapid spread into the private sphere as well after prices dropped in the early 1980s, this profit motive and consumer demand went hand in hand in producing ever more refined versions to fit expressed needs outside the business world as well as within. The matter of more comprehensive internal dictionaries, for example, which did not contain a wider lexical spread than that dictated solely by office needs, and the provision of fonts which mimicked handwriting to address the concerns of coldness in printed text exemplify this symbiotic relationship. If manufacturers had not been convinced by the kind of escalating sales trajectories described in Chapter One that meeting such requests would result in a profit for themselves, the technology might well have withered on the vine or remained in its initial stage of development. "New consumer products are not called out of the air by consumer demands: they are the result of suppliers, in various industries, seeking to establish products that will capture a slice of household expenditures ... And even those products which have been established in the market are frequently subject to continuing innovation, to make them more attractive to consumers vis-à-vis competitors for money – especially competition from products with similar functions." (Miles et al, 1992: 67) Economic imperatives rooted deeply in Japan's business and social infrastructure have thus driven not only the initial development of this technology but also its subsequent ongoing refinement.

In no sense, therefore, has this technology developed independently of the society in which it functions; it has been linked inextricably with its profitability to large corporations. Wajcman (1994: 6) sums it up thus: "If ... technological systems are economic enterprises, and if they are involved directly or indirectly in market competition, then technical change is forced on them. If they are to survive at all, and even prosper, they cannot forever stand still. Technical change is made inevitable, and its nature and direction profoundly conditioned by this. And when national economies are linked by a competitive world market, technological change outside a particular country can exert massive pressure for technological change inside it." A similar technology had been developed in western countries, which did not face the difficulties of the large character set, many years earlier, providing a powerful impetus to Japan to "catch up" in terms of office automation, as we shall see.

But has the availability of the technology itself somehow changed Japanese society? There are strong perceptions that the nature of the way in which the script is used are changing as a result of the ability to retrieve characters electronically, and that interpersonal relations are also changing as a result of the increasing displacement of handwriting. Then of course there is the growth in Internet use that the technology has made possible. Whether these taken together add up to social change at this stage is arguable. If, however, word processor use escalates to the point at which it impacts on national script policy, as discussed in Chapter Three, then the resultant ramifications for education and the printing industry will certainly be definable as both quantitative and qualitative social change.

This book examines the initial development of this technology and its subsequent rapid dissemination in Japan, with an eye to both the practical and the affective changes its use has brought and continues to bring. All of these, up to and including Internet use, have been driven not solely by consumer demand but by the underlying profit motive. Chapter One begins by outlining the patterns of growth of the new technology and considers the reasons for that growth, including the nature of the Japanese script itself. I discuss efforts to develop a typewriter in Japan and reasons why they were, if not unsuccessful, at least unsatisfactory. The local implications of word processing technology are examined. Chapter Two describes the technology itself, investigating early attempts to achieve document production by machine and the changes which the word processor brought about in the office and home. Chapter Three proceeds to an examination of what the perceived changes attributed to use of the word processor are, and what the possible contours of Japan's future script policy might be. Finally, Chapter Four explores the cultural consequences of the technology for both the lives of its users and the wider society in which they operate, investigating its significance for interpersonal communication values, approaches to writing, work habits and Japan's presence on the Internet.

This book does not seek to discuss the basic technical aspects of how characters are handled electronically; that has already been done in Lunde's *Understanding Japanese Information Processing* (1993) and is in any case beyond my expertise. What I discuss is the development and the subsequent social impact of the technology, and the capacity of its users to construct a meaningful relationship with it as it challenges accepted habits and values relating to orthographic practice and its associated contexts. I have tried wherever possible to let the voices of those involved in the debate speak for themselves, so that the discourse comes from those most intimately concerned.

Throughout the book the term "word processor" or "word processing technology" is used to refer to both stand-alone word processors (machines which can only be used for this purpose) and to word processing software for the personal computer. For the first decade of its existence we shall see that it was mainly the former that dominated the market and may even have delayed the spread of the latter. Since around 1992, however, the personal computer has caught up. I make no claim to have mentioned all the types of word processor or input methods or even of typewriters available, just the major representative ones which carry the debate forward and highlight areas of significance.

A final note: Japanese names are given in Japanese order, ie surname first. I have left very often used Japanese words such as kanji, kana, hiragana and katakana unmarked, as to italicise or underline them makes a visually unappealing text. Less common Japanese words are italicised, except that where a word forms part of a sentence or grammatical explanation it is left unmarked and enclosed in quote marks.

CHAPTER ONE

From Manuscript to Monitor

One of the major success stories of Japanese technology during the 1980s was the invention and marketing of word processing technology. This technology had developed much earlier in western countries, where the alphabet posed no significant difficulty, but was for a long time thought impossible in Japan because of the nature of the Japanese writing system. It was not until 1978 that Toshiba succeeded in producing a word processor capable of handling both input and output using characters. In the early 1980s, the technology came within the reach of the average consumer, thanks to rapid advances in the field that led to price falls. There followed an exponentially increasing rise in sales, not just in the business sector but also in the sphere of personal use. This book will tell the story of that growth and its consequences, charting the rapid spread of the technology and its considerable impact on the business, orthographic and cultural practices of its users.

The issue of how to reproduce characters either mechanically on typewriters or electronically on word processors is not of course unique to Japan. It has vexed other countries in East Asia as well, notably China and Korea, both of which have also arrived at electronic solutions. We shall see in Chapter Five some of the difficulties with uniform standards which still remain throughout the East Asian region. This book, however, will deal primarily with Japan's own solution to the problem. It will present the story of the development and consequences of a technology long desired, rapidly diffused and now enabling Japan to construct a global presence through the Internet.

Patterns of growth

Let me begin by dazzling my readers with sales statistics, which show us clearly how rapidly word processing technology was accepted in Japan after it became available at prices most could afford. The boom in sales of stand-alone word processor units began around 1984. Figure 1 shows the annual sales figures recorded by the Ministry of International Trade and Industry (MITI) between 1982 and 1986. We can see that the really big surges took place in 1984, 1985 and 1986, as advances in computer technology and economies of scale made possible by mass production combined to lower prices. At around this time, words like personal computer, word processor and database came into common use in everyday discourse; the word *waapuro* or *wapuro* (short for *waado purosessaa*, the Japanese equivalent of 'word processor') figured prominently in speech and writing as debate about the new writing technology escalated. So often were the stand-alone machines advertised, one writer commented wryly as early as 1983, that the advertisements made the national dailies look like trade papers for the electronics business (Sakai 1983: 3). One year later, another observed that it would by then be rare to find someone who did not have a word processor in the home or in the workplace (Fujisaki 1984: 111). That was clearly an exaggeration, but the perception nevertheless reflects community astonishment at the popularity of the new machine. The same writer predicted an increase in sales figures from 300,000 in 1984 to an estimated one million by the end of 1986. In fact, the MITI figures given in Figure 1 show that the 1986 sales were more than double this estimate.

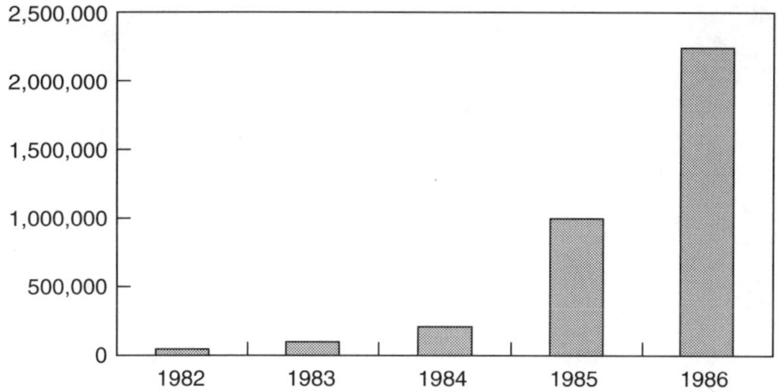

Figure 1: word processor units sold 1982–1986 (Source: Tsūsan Daijin Kanbō Chōsa Tōkeibu 1987: 226)

By 1986, 90% of businesses were using word processing to produce Japanese-language documents (Tsūsan Daijin Kanbō Chōsa Tōkeibu 1986: 448). Of the total number of word processors in circulation the following year, however, close to 90% were for personal as opposed to office use. Citing an Asahi Shinbun article from April that year which reported that close to three million families owned a word processor, researcher Endō Orie calculated that on the basis of government figures for the number of households in Japan, that meant about one in twelve households. This study further found that prices and functions had also changed to the extent that companies now changed models about every six months (Endō et al 1987: 63). By the beginning of 1991, a survey by the Economic Planning Agency found that one in four people possessed a word processor (Aoyama 1991: 217). Later figures for the 1991 financial year indicate that 32.6% of all households owned a word processor that year; by 1993, this had risen to 37.8% of all households (see Figure 2).

Once the perception of students as a potential market took hold in the mid-'80s, prices dropped still further, but at the same time the range of available functions increased. Word

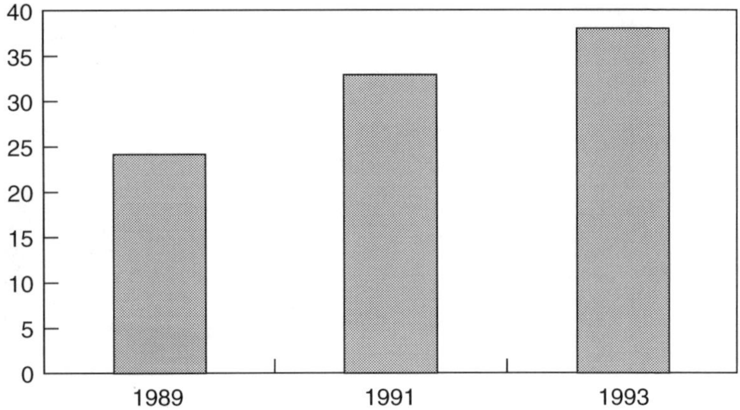

Figure 2: % of households owning word processors 1989–1993 (Source: Japan Statistical Association 1992: 548 and 1995: 588)

processors and computers using word processing software then began to make their impact felt in schools and universities as well, with an increasing number of institutions requiring student assignments to be printed out rather than handwritten. By 1993, a Tokyo survey revealed, 20.5% of primary-school students and 22% of middle- and high-school students had computers at home, while 47.3% of primary-school students and 46.3% of middle- and high-school students had stand-alone word processors (Nakajima 1993: 666).

The opening of the Japanese market to American computer companies began with the 'Compaq-shock' in 1992 when clones made by Compaq arrived in Japan at half the price of the local NEC machines. This has increased the number of those who prefer to use word-processing software on a PC rather than a stand-alone word processor, seeking both the wider range of applications a PC allows and, more recently, Internet access. Figure 3 compares households owning stand-alone word processors and personal computers between 1988 and 1997; by 1994, the PC component was beginning to increase, though many more households owned word

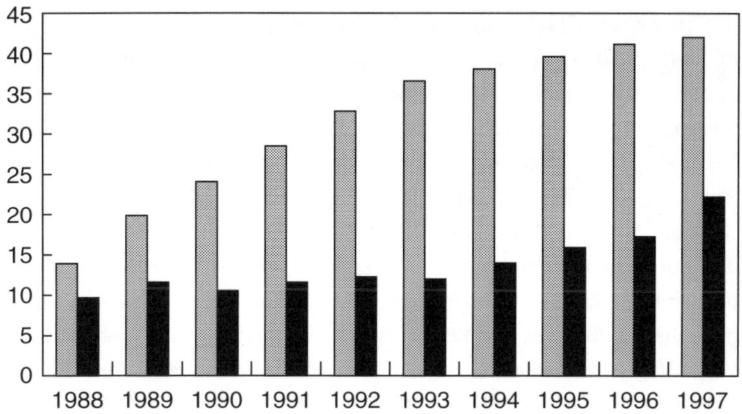

Figure 3: comparison of households with word processors and personal computers, 1988–1997 (Source: Economic Planning Agency 1997)

processors than PCs. Note that these figures are for ownership, not annual sales – there is nothing to tell us when the word processors were bought; many may have been bought as much as several years earlier. If we look at actual sales figures, we find that annual sales of stand-alone word processors peaked in 1991 at 2.6 million units. In 1994, PC sales surpassed those of word processors for the first time by a large margin (1,123,900,000,000 yen as compared to 187,100,000,000 yen), prompting Abe Keisuke to speculate in the Asahi Yearbook that 1994 would eventually become known as *pasokon gannen* (the first year of the PC's reign). The following year, annual sales of word processors dropped below two million for the first time in ten years (Abe 1995: 290).

The first half of the 1990s, then, saw growth in the sector of word processing packages used on PCs at the expense of the stand-alone word processor, although the latter continued to be popular because of its easy portability and all-inclusive nature. Japanese companies began to invest more in information technology about this time, and the PC also began to spread widely among individual users, spurred by interest in the Internet. (There is still a long way to go, however, before PC diffusion in Japan rises to the levels found in America and Australia: in 1997 only around 20% of Japanese had PCs, compared to over 40% in the United States and about 35% in Australia.) (International Telecommunication Union, 1998). The early 1990s also saw the appearance of Japanese versions of Word Perfect, Word and other word processing software for use on these computers, starting with the release of a Japanese version of Windows 3.0 in 1991. Japan also began to establish a sizeable presence on the Internet, after a slow start caused by confusion among the ministries responsible for national communications policy. By July 1998, JP top-level domain names ranked fifth in the number of hosts supported on the Internet (Network Wizards, July 1998), and as of August 1998, the Japanese language was the second most widely used language other than English on the Internet after Spanish (Global Internet Statistics 1998). Japanese language versions of different kinds of software have proliferated, including Internet packages: the Japanese version of Internet Explorer 5, for example, was released in March 1999. None of this rapid growth in Japan's presence on the Internet would have been possible without the invention of word processing technology.

Why the script delayed the technology

What lies behind the astonishingly rapid spread of this technology both within and outside the business world? Part of the answer lies in the novelty of the technology itself, in that for the first time the long-standing and seemingly intractable problem of how to produce printed documents in Japanese had been addressed in an effective and realistic manner. Perhaps the best way to appreciate the significance of this breakthrough is to compare the English-language experience with that in Japan.

Ten years ago, when I wrote for publication, I wrote in longhand which was later typed up on an electronic typewriter. Since then, along with just about everyone else I know, I have progressed to using a computer word processing program which enables me to create, edit and print a document with much greater ease and in a much shorter time. It never occurs to me that there is anything particularly remarkable about the process: I simply take it for granted that if I type in the letters r-e-m-a-r-k-a-b-l-e, the word 'remarkable' will appear immediately on the screen and eventually in the printed text. And indeed, there is little to wonder at, in the case of languages such as English that use an alphabet, that input so readily translates into output.

When a document produced on a Japanese word processor rolls out of its printer, however, it represents a significant victory over considerable obstacles. The reason, of course, lies in the nature of the Japanese script. Modern Japanese is written using a combination of three scripts: kanji (Chinese characters) and two phonetic scripts, hiragana and katakana. This situation came about because characters, imported around fifteen hundred years ago from China in the absence of any native orthography, could not be used efficiently on their own to write Japanese; they had originally been developed to suit the requirements of a language with markedly different features (see Miller 1980 for further details). The two phonetic scripts were therefore eventually developed in Japan to address the problem of how to indicate not only the pronunciation of Japanese words (which of course the Chinese characters could not do) but also the verbal and adjectival inflections and postpositions not found in Chinese. Both scripts now represent the same forty-six short syllables.

Over the centuries, texts have been written in varying combinations of the three scripts. Today, Japanese texts are written in a blend of Chinese characters, hiragana representing native grammatical features or in certain words which convention decrees are not written with characters, and katakana for foreign loanwords, foreign names (other than those of Chinese origin), domestic telegrams (when those were still in use) and for emphasis. While there are many thousands of characters available, the current script policy document of the National Language Council recommends 1,945 of the most commonly occurring for general use, and these are the guidelines followed by the Education Ministry in schools. In practice, around 3,000–3,500 characters are needed to read newspapers, advertisements and other sources of text encountered in daily life (Seeley 1991: 2; Tanaka 1991: 59–60).

A simple example will illustrate how this system works and will lead us to an understanding of why machine production of documents has until recently proved so difficult in Japan. Take the sentence

キャンベラという都市はオーストラリアの首都です。

Kyanbera to iu toshi wa Ōsutoraria no shuto desu

Canberra is the capital city of Australia.

Here 'toshi' and 'shuto' are nouns meaning 'city' and 'capital city' respectively; 'Kyanbera' and 'Ōsutoraria' are proper nouns giving the name of a city and a country; 'to iu' indicates that the name of the city referred to is Canberra; 'wa' is a case marker indicating that the word which precedes it is the topic of the sentence; 'no' is a possessive marker; and 'desu' is the verb 'to be', meaning in this context 'it is'. As can be seen from the Japanese version, 'Kyanbera' and 'Ōsutoraria' are written in the angular katakana script because they are foreign place names; 'toshi' and 'shuto', both nouns, are written with characters; and the grammatical particles, 'to iu' and the copula are written in hiragana. In order to write this sentence by hand, one must remember and correctly reproduce four characters interspersed with hiragana; write two words in katakana; and remember that the particle 'wa', in a carryover of prewar usage, is traditionally written with the symbol for 'ha'.

Suppose the sentence had included a verb other than the copula, such as for instance:

よくコーヒーを飲みます。

yoku kōhii o nomimasu

I often drink coffee

Here, the first syllable of the word 'nomimasu' ([I] drink) is written with the kanji logograph for 'drink', and the remainder of the word, including the non-past suffix, is written in hiragana. The adverb 'yoku' (often) is these days also written in hiragana. So is the object-marker postposition 'o', although it is traditionally written with the symbol for 'wo', the only use to which this particular symbol is now put. While there is a certain amount of free play involved in the substitution of hiragana for characters, depending on context, these simple examples demonstrate what has become the clearly defined pattern for the interwoven use of the three scripts in postwar Japan. 'Kōhii', a loanword, is written in katakana.

Navigating the interplay between the three scripts in writing by hand, intricate though it seems to onlookers, poses no particular difficulty for Japanese themselves once they have learned the system. The two phonetic scripts present no particular challenge, being simple to learn and to use. What can seem problematic is the use of Chinese characters, specifically the burden on memory produced by the aggregate of the size of the character set and the multiplicity of its uses (one character may have several different pronunciations depending on the context in which it occurs). In writing by hand, one faces issues such as remembering the correct number of strokes in a character in the correct spatial relationship, recognising which of several similar characters is used in a particular word, and in general being able to call up from memory the required characters, however many they may be. To those of us used to a 26-letter alphabet, the task of having to remember a couple of thousand differently-shaped characters, often with common elements in different combinations, can seem daunting. Millions of Japanese manage it on a daily basis, however, as a natural and almost automatic process, equating the thought necessary to decide on a particular point in doubt with regard to a character with that necessary to be sure of the correct spelling of a word in English. Despite the dire warnings of those who believed that the Japanese script constituted a severe handicap to progress (see Gottlieb 1995), Japan has managed to reach its present prominent position without being noticeably handicapped by its orthography.

In all aspects but one, that is. The office automation revolution in the form of new document production techniques which occurred in the West with the development of the typewriter and later the word processor found Japan unable to compete in this area because of the input-output difficulty posed by the script. A Japanese typewriter (at first for kana only but later including characters as well) was developed but was bulky and laborious to use, requiring specialist training for effective use. Instead of being able to key in text quickly as on an English-language typewriter, the Japanese typist had to first locate and then retrieve the desired character from a large matrix of metal characters, a much more time-consuming process. The size of the character set also meant that the machine could not be easily moved around. To return to our first example sentence above: to type this using a Japanese typewriter would involve finding and retrieving a total of twenty-two symbols from three different matrices and would take much longer to type than the romanised version of the sentence.

The 'typewriter age'

How was business (in the sense of document production) conducted in a Japanese office before the advent of word processing technology? Mostly by hand, because of the nature of the script and the consequent problems for input and output. The fax machine was developed as one way around the problem of input (Unger 1987: 165; Kodama 1991: 13) but not, of course, of output. Typing skills were not part of the duties of the ordinary office worker but were reserved for specially trained operators. Work which needed to be presented in a neater form was sent to specialist typists, either inside the company or outside contractors.

At Bishika Shisutemu, an information processing service company set up in 1970 as part of the Mitsubishi Chemicals group, for example, despite an increase in the volume of office work as business activities increased, the company did not buy more Japanese typewriters. Instead, it sent contracts and a small number of documents which it deemed needed typing to subcontractors outside the company. All the rest of the general documents were done by hand, with female staff members in charge of making clean copies of everything. This meant that as the volume of business increased, there developed a noticeable time lag between the writing of a draft and the making of its clean copy. As well, typing subcontractors often could not supply documents by the due date because of the need for revision and retyping (Nihon Jōhō Shori Kaihatsu Kyōkai 1981: 76).

For writers, the process of having a manuscript printed involved writing the original by hand on squared manuscript paper and sending it to an editor. The editor would pencil in corrections, clear them with the writer, and send the (still handwritten and often by now partly illegible) document to the printer, who would then face the difficult task of deciphering both the original handwriting and the editorial additions. In 1984, the majority of manuscripts given to printers in Japan were still handwritten. Although most were overscored with additions, in less than perfect handwriting, and were in general hard to read, the printer was expected to accept them without complaint. By contrast, in the United States, manuscripts sent to printers were usually typewritten and much easier to handle (Tatsuoka 1984: 4).

When former editor Fujita Ryōichi became head of production at the respected journal Chūō Kōron in 1969, he was surprised to discover how much of that department's work was being done by hand. Fujita believed that much of the office work ought to be done by machine instead, in particular such jobs as verifications and ledger postings which did not require decision-making. He therefore introduced a punch card system and began to look into the development of an improved version of a kana typewriter. Red-pencilled corrections made in the editorial section, Fujita knew from his own previous experience as an editor, were meant to help the printers read the manuscript. When he moved to the production department, however, he was surprised at the extent of the difficulty which handwritten manuscripts caused the printers. Even with the revisions in red, the manuscripts were often illegible because of poor, minuscule or idiosyncratic handwriting. Sometimes printers even returned them as impossible to handle. If the editorial section criticised the printers for the number of misprints, the blame would often be laid on the illegibility of the characters in the first place. Clearly, the printery needed clean copy of manuscripts, but for the editors to achieve this involved large amounts of time and trouble. Handwritten clean copies were considered the only option; the Japanese typewriter was too inefficient in terms of time. Fujita did experiment with typing a manuscript on his kana typewriter and underlining the places where he wanted kanji substituted for kana, but the printers rejected this idea as impracticable, in no small part because they felt the unfamiliar horizontally-written text slowed them down in collecting pieces of type (Umesao 1988: 179,182–84).

Vocal romanisation advocate Yamada Hisao once proposed the rather novel idea that the complexity of Japan's writing system was a contributing factor both to the concentration of Japanese industry in the Tokyo and Osaka areas (as opposed to the provincial decentralisation which often occurred in Europe and the United States following the Industrial Revolution) and to the development of the Japanese management style. Of course, the concentration of industry in these areas occurred because of other factors such as centralised government, the need to be near ports for imports of materials, and the fact that these two cities were already centres of production, commerce and consumption. Yamada suggested, however, that it was also because the transmission of information in document form was made so difficult by the nature of the script that more face-to-face personal contact in commerce and industry was required in Japan than elsewhere. American and European business styles, which until then had not been all that different from those in Japan, had begun to develop along a divergent path after the appearance of the typewriter in the United States in the 1870s led to the creation of a class of employees such as secretaries and typists who specialised in handling document production. American statistics showed that close to 20% of the population were people whose daily jobs involved using a keyboard to handle text. A rough idea of their productivity could be gained by reflecting that a manuscript formerly written by hand in an hour could be neatly typed up in ten or at the most fifteen minutes. This was the secret of America's high white collar productivity: the perfection of these documents and the establishment of the line of command. In short, Yamada proposed, the lack of a similar typewriter in Japan, consequent upon the complexity of the script, changed the entire business management ethos of the nation (Yamada 1984: 4–5, 9).

This startling thesis accords the script somewhat more prominence in the overall scheme of business and industry than is really due. It is certainly true, however, that the Japanese typewriter was not efficient in terms of output relative to time spent. Why was that? The first of these machines (known in Japanese as the *wabun taipu*, or the *kana kanji majiribun taipu*) had not been invented until 1915 by Sugimoto Kyota (Murata 1958: 18). A Japanese typewriter had no keyboard; there were far too many symbols to make a keyboard practicable. Instead, pieces of movable type were packed in a tray in front of the operator. The trays contained the two phonetic kana script symbols, several thousand kanji, Arabic numerals, and numerous other symbols. In some models, the western alphabet was also included. In order to print a character, the operator had to retrieve it from this large set by first locating it and picking it up with a movable arm. The character could then be printed, not by striking through a ribbon with a key as in the case of the western typewriter but by hitting the paper directly with the inked piece of metal type itself, which was then replaced in the tray. This process was repeated with each character. As a result of the multiplicity of pieces of metal type required, the machine was both bulky and heavy, certainly not portable. The operator needed strong arms and shoulders – quite a deal of strength was needed to get a clear print with each piece of movable type, and the process entailed a fair amount of noise. The machines were also expensive: by 1981, a Japanese typewriter sold for between 250,000 and 300,000 yen (Nihon Jōhō Shori Kaihatsu Kyōkai 1981: 55). The expense, added to their size and lack of portability, meant that they were found mostly in companies and offices rather than in the studies of private persons, again contrasting with the portable typewriter in the west which was widely used by the general public.

Touch typing, of course, was out of the question, as the operator needed visual confirmation that each piece was the correct one before selecting it, and there was no keyboard on which both hands of the typist could be deployed. The cost of input in terms of both time and consequently operator's salary was therefore much more than in the case of the western typewriter. The time taken to locate a character in the tray slowed down the production of text. A page of A4 paper could be typed in 30 minutes on a Japanese typewriter, as opposed to 20 minutes if it were written by hand. To carry out a partial revision of about 180 characters on the page took the same amount of time for both because both the handwritten and the typed documents had to be completely redone (Nihon Jōhō Shori Kaihatsu Kyōkai 1981: 90). In terms of characters per minute, Toshiba's Mori Ken'ichi, who played a leading role in the development of the first Japanese word processor, found that the Japanese typewriter could produce around 30 cpm compared to the 70cpm of handwriting (Tanaka 1991: 29). The need to retype the whole document if changes were made added to the time involved. People often wished to make changes to a typed-up document, but because of the pressure of schedules, the documents were only retyped in special cases (Nihon Jōhō Shori Kaihatsu Kyōkai 1981: 81).

A machine of this nature was thus too slow to be practicable as a machine for intellectual production, meaning a machine on which one could actually compose text and type it out at the same time without first making a handwritten draft. Rather, because of the nature of the script, it was restricted to the production of clean copy of handwritten documents by specialists, whereas the typewriter in the United States had evolved with time and the development of touch typing from a mere clean copy machine to a machine which people could use to compose as they went.

The nature of the Japanese typist's job was thus continuous specialised operation of the machine rather than a mix of typing with other office duties as elsewhere. The image of the typist was of someone apart from other office workers, in the sense of a clear division of roles between writing documents and typing them (Mori, Yamane et al. 1988: 8). Whereas in the west it was expected as a matter of course that secretaries were able to type, in Japan secretaries and typists were generally separate categories with skills that were not interchangeable. The situation could not have been more different from that in the west, where in terms of business practice (and often elsewhere) 'to write' had long since come to mean 'to type' and where it was rare for letters or documents to be handwritten because using a typewriter was conspicuously more effective.

To those who wanted to reform the Japanese script by getting rid of characters, the limitations of the typewriter presented a heaven-sent opportunity for criticism of the script, usually formulated in terms of social and national disadvantage. The anti-kanji camp for many years after the war made it their main argument that office automation would never be possible unless Japan stopped using characters and adopted the alphabet. To give an example of a representative comment: surely, one romanisation advocate's argument ran, the basis of a real democracy is the ability of each individual to communicate ideas with ease and openness to the rest of society. In other countries, typewriters allowed even complete amateurs to produce pamphlets fairly easily using a typewriter, but in Japan one could not do this without time, effort and special training. This made a somewhat empty cant of the idea of free exchange of opinions towards a new Japan (Saitō 1989: 23). The lack of a typewriter was linked strongly with notions that the intellectual life of the country itself suffered because of this.

The kana typewriters

As will be clear from the Fujita story mentioned above, the kanji typewriter was not the only version of the typewriter used in Japan. Those who viewed kanji rather than the phonetic syllabaries as the root cause of the input problem promoted the use of the kana-only typewriter.

The **katakana typewriter**, first to be invented, was the brainchild of Sumitomo executive Yamashita Yoshitarō, who in 1920 founded the Kanamojikai (Kana Society) dedicated to working for the abolition of kanji and the promotion of katakana as the national script. Yamashita had spent some years abroad as a diplomat, during which time he came to the conclusion that what he perceived as Japan's comparative backwardness in culture was due to its script. In or about 1921, his friend Hoshino Yukinori, a Kansai industrialist, visited the American Underwood Typewriter Company with a view to developing a katakana typewriter for the Japanese market. By chance, at Underwood, Hoshino met a linguist fluent in several languages including Japanese, who was familiar with Japanese script. Following initial discussions between Hoshino and this man, Yamashita also met with him to discuss the idea. As a result, the first Underwood katakana typewriters were imported into Japan in 1923 (Toyota 1989: 513–14). These machines had keyboards and typed horizontally in katakana, which at the time was more widely used in combination with kanji than hiragana and was taught before hiragana in schools. Many authors still used katakana with kanji in their manuscripts, as was also the practice in official documents and Imperial Rescripts. The hiragana-kanji mix was gaining ground, however, in newspapers, magazines and other areas; by 1946, when the new constitution was written in hiragana-kanji, it had become more commonly used and familiar than katakana, which was a strike against the katakana typewriter.

Katakana typewriters were used mainly as billing machines in large companies. They were not marketed as 'writing machines', and little effort was put into promoting this aspect of their use (Ishida 1982: 12). Even telexes in katakana were rewritten to include kanji before being presented to superiors, a practice involving a singular waste of time which arose because those of lower status in the office hierarchy felt obligated to use kanji. An interesting sidelight on this preference for kanji is that blind people used katakana typewriters. While society at large was not ready to accept a change from kanji to katakana, non-sighted people were not visually attached to kanji and therefore had no particular motivation to continue using them (Tsukahara 1982: 210).

One disadvantage of the katakana typewriter was that although these machines were unique to Japan, there was no standardisation among the keyboards of the various models. JIS (the Japan Industrial Standards organisation) had certified three different layouts; the Navy had a different, and, some believed, superior one again. Nor was the typewriter keyboard layout the same as that of the teletype. This caused some inconvenience to companies, who had to employ separate typists for the teletype and for the office katakana typewriter (and also, presumably, for the kanji typewriter if they had one). In large companies with many employees this might not have been so much of a problem. Smaller companies, however, wanted their keyboard operators to be able to use both systems, particularly in view of the fact that the telex was only used for a couple of hours a day at most in most medium and small businesses. The typist was expected to be using a different typewriter for the remaining working hours, but this was made harder than it needed to be by the layout difference. The obvious solution was to standardise the katakana keyboard to that of the telex; there would be no point in doing it the other way round, given the multiplicity of layouts in the typewriter and the fact that unless all telex boards were identical, no communication could take place between them (Saitō 1989: 32–33).

Despite this drawback, however, which came down to a matter of manufacturers each promoting special features of their own machine in order to set it apart from others, Murata Takao, writing in 1958 on the present use and future outlook of the katakana typewriter, was able to marshal a battery of convincing arguments in its favour. Handwriting letters, he contended, put a great deal of strain on the writer's wrist and led everyone to develop idiosyncratic, often hard to decipher writing styles. The kanji typewriter was an attempt to remedy this situation, true, but it was ultimately rendered ineffective by the complexity of the character set. The keyboard-based katakana typewriter, however, could be used at three times the speed of the kanji typewriter (30cpm for the kanji typewriter and 100 cpm for the katakana typewriter). As 70% of office work involved writing, this three-to-one difference was quite important. Then there were the other advantages, such as lack of personal idiosyncrasies in the text (unlike handwritten texts) and ease of making carbon copies. The input problem, Murata considered, was solved by the katakana typewriter; the remaining problem was its output. People who were accustomed to reading vertically-written text incorporating kanji found it difficult to read horizontally-written katakana text quickly. This, however, he viewed as only a minor hindrance which would pass as people in time became more familiar with the practice.

There followed a list of places which were using the katakana typewriter for office work requiring the generation of multiple accounts, the reproduction of a lot of figures, and the use of many foreign loanwords. Government offices such as the Self-Defence Forces and over 130 municipal offices including the city halls of Osaka and Fukuoka, banks such as Fuji and Mitsui, insurance companies such as Yasuda and Tokyo, securities companies such as Nomura, electricity and gas companies, textile and printing companies - the list spanned a wide cross-section of the business world. The katakana typewriter was used in these institutions for salary payments, accounts, bank money orders and share certificates, to list but a few of its applications. It was also used in the various branches of the insurance business for tasks which required many figures and proper nouns. In 1958, Murata calculated, there were close to 10,000 such typewriters in use; he listed the numbers found in large companies such as Tokyo Electric, which used 200 machines to send out electricity accounts to each household. All enterprises he surveyed mentioned a marked increase in efficiency, and further reported that although the katakana-only text had initially been hard to read, they now would not consider giving it up.

Municipal offices used the katakana typewriter mainly for water rates notices. The biggest was Hiroshima, which in September 1952 possessed seven machines. When the machines were first introduced, an operator would average 400-500 notices per day, which was about the same as handwriting. After eight months of using the typewriters, however, this figure had increased to 1,800 notices per day per operator. In Osaka, similarly dealing with water rates notices, the use of the typewriters resulted in the number of personnel employed in these operations being reduced from

82 to 40. Despite this, the number of rates notices produced per month jumped from 180,000 to 200,000. The savings thus effected over one year totalled more than ten million yen. Other companies reported similar success stories, including the Daiichi Bank which had previously used the kanji typewriter and found the katakana typewriter three times more efficient in terms of output, with less training needed. With the horizontal kanji typewriter, for bills of exchange, a trained operator would need 60–70 seconds per item. With the katakana typewriter, even someone who had only finished their basic training two or three months earlier could produce one in 35–40 seconds; with further experience, this diminished to 25–30 seconds. To produce a handwritten bill would require 50–90 seconds, and a day spent in this labour would result in fatigue. To handle around five hundred of these bills of exchange per day, on a basis of two employees either writing by hand or using the kanji typewriter, would require extra overtime. If the number were closer to a thousand, even with three or four operators assigned to the task, the overtime bill would still be high. With the katakana typewriter, however, no extra people and only a little overtime were needed to handle the same volume of work. The katakana typewriter tired its operator physically much less than the kanji typewriter, and was, overall, three times faster.

Of course there were a couple of drawbacks. One was the difficulty of distinguishing between the many homophones of Japanese. Kanji provided visual clues as to which was meant, whereas the phonetic kana did not. Another was the need to put spaces between words in the correct places to prevent misreading (when kanji were used, Japanese was normally written without such spaces). One message sent requesting that a pilot be sent early to a ship was mistakenly read as 'don't send the pilot' (*hayame ni*, early, being understood as ... *wa yame ni*), with the result that the ship was kept waiting. Then there was the problem of deciding on the correct, often idiosyncratic pronunciations for proper nouns such as personal and place names. Such problems could be overcome with time and training and were not seen as detracting from the main benefit offered by the katakana typewriter, that of freeing personnel to do other work by releasing them from the type of mechanical task best done by machines (Murata 1958: 18–25).

Despite this optimistic outlook, the problem of the appearance of the printed katakana text was not to be so easily overcome. While katakana input was certainly much easier than kanji, the output was much harder to read for people accustomed to reading kanji-hiragana text. Ten years later, unwillingness to read katakana-only text was still seen as a drawback which made the katakana typewriter suitable only for short letters rather than for longer documents, unless one were an expert in the field to which the documents pertained. An experiment was conducted at the Japan Science and Technology Information Centre with the aim of testing the claim that katakana were hard to read. Staff members from the Centre, specialists in metal engineering, were divided into three groups, shown a manuscript written in katakana, and asked to rewrite it incorporating kanji within a specified short time limit. It was expected that there would be mistakes in converting it back to kanji, but in fact, when the average of the conversion rate for the three groups was taken (ie the proportion of correct conversions in the total), it proved to be 98.8% correct. If one were a specialist in a given area, it seemed, one could read katakana text perfectly well, inferring the meaning of any problematic words from the context; a katakana typewriter would therefore serve well for any such specialist wishing to avoid the labour of kanji input (Miyabara, Takeuchi et al. 1968: 20,22). For the non-specialist reader, however, it was a different matter: the katakana text was much less easily read.

A **katakana-romaji (roman alphabet) combination typewriter** was also available. First designed by Ogata Tomio using a combination keyboard on Maruzen's Royal typewriter in 1929, it was properly launched after the end of World War

Two and was highly praised for the convenience of the combination of katakana with the internationally accepted alphabet. This machine sold better than the exclusively katakana typewriter. As in the case of the katakana-only typewriter, however, there was no standardisation of keyboards, so that the combination typewriter came with almost a different layout for every machine. A survey of all katakana typewriters put out by the Nihon Jimu Nōritsu Kyōkai (Japan Office Efficiency Organisation) defended this on the grounds that the frequency of use of the various letters depended on what the typewriter was being used for and that therefore it was only natural that each keyboard should be different. This line of argument drew criticism from one writer, who commented caustically that if this were the case one might have thought that manufacturers would specify what particular line of work their own layout had been designed for. His own close perusal of numerous catalogues had led him to the conclusion that the focus was on denigration of other brands of typewriter rather than any explanation as to the rationale behind the manufacturer's particular keyboard. Perhaps the makers were afraid that specifying their product would narrow their market, although he dismissed this as a sales technique more suited to the feudal period than to the internationally competitive present. In the west, he noted, where typewriters had become a part of everyday life, keyboard layouts were the same regardless of how the machine was used, so that everybody was able to use the same machine with ease (Saitō 1989: 21).

After the war, as a result of changes in script, hiragana replaced katakana as the most widely used phonetic script; katakana were relegated by and large to foreign loanwords, telegrams and a few other limited uses. In 1956, Kōza Nihongo published the results of a questionnaire on language-related issues in which support for hiragana outweighed support for katakana by a factor of four to one (Saitō 1989: 16). It was only to be expected, then, that manufacture of a **hiragana typewriter** would soon begin, and in fact the first such machine appeared in 1962. It was developed in Kyoto by Saitō Kyōzō in collaboration with Kawakami Akira, an instructor at the Supreme Court in Tokyo who had invented a *sokutaipu* shorthand machine for making court records. Kawakami and Saitō had twenty sets of hiragana type made (Umesao 1988: 170).

Several companies began manufacturing typewriters which produced horizontally-written hiragana text around 1971. At one stage, Chūō Kōron's Fujita and Umesao Tadao had attempted to convince the Brother company, which in 1970 was making 500,000 typewriters a year and exporting 90% of them, to develop what they called the KANAkana typewriter. This would incorporate keys for hiragana, katakana and the alphabet, would operate by a system of three shift keys, and would be the only machine in the world to type vertically. A prototype was made in 1973, but later production was halted by Brother's decision in 1975 not to proceed, the company being reluctant to outlay funds on production after the 1973 oil shock in case the machines did not sell well. The idea of a typewriter which combined all three phonetic scripts in one machine thus did not get off the ground. In 1978, the first Japanese word processor, which instead took technology in a direction which reaffirmed the central position of kanji to Japanese script, was exhibited at a trade fair in Tokyo, and it was not long before Brother brought out its own version, prompting Umesao to conjecture that their prior experience in designing his KANAkana typewriter may have helped the Brother technicians in doing this (1988: 150–205).

There were various views in circulation concerning the relative efficiency of the kana (whether hiragana or katakana) typewriter and the alphabet typewriter. One common perception was that the kana typewriter, because of the C-V syllabic structure of Japanese, was twice as fast as the alphabet typewriter because most keys typed a single C-V syllable which would take two keys to type with the alphabet. For example, the kana symbol for 'ka' would require only one stroke on the kana typewriter but two on the alphabet typewriter. Ogata Zyun'iti, a doctor who was a member of the Romanisation Society, tested this claim by typing the same sentences in both scripts and counting the number of times the keys were struck. He found that the proportion of kana symbols to romaji letters was 1:1.69, but that the proportion of keystrokes on the kana typewriter to those on the romaji typewriter was 1:1.37 where the use of the shift key was counted as 1, 1:1.34 where it was counted as two and 1:1.29 where it was counted as three. The shift key might be counted as more than one because it took more work to operate it than to strike an ordinary key, and because it was necessary to use it to access certain symbols on the kana typewriter. The shift key use as a proportion of total key use in the test was 4.4% in romaji text and 7.9% in kana text. In the light of these results, Ogata deduced, the kana typewriter was more efficient than the romaji typewriter in a ratio of about 1:1.3, ie a sentence which took ten minutes to type on a kana typewriter would take thirteen minutes on a romaji machine.

There were, however, several caveats attached to these findings. For a start, the kana typewriter had 46 keys, compared to only 21 on the romaji version. Eight of these keys carried two symbols each, which made the use of the kana typewriter more difficult in terms of psychological burden. Nine of the kana typewriter keys required the use of the weaker little finger, compared to only three on the romaji typewriter; moreover, the shift key, which required strength, had to be used 1.8 times more often on the kana typewriter. A typist's fingers would therefore tire more easily on that machine. Furthermore, on the kana typewriter, the distance between the guide key in the centre row and the keys used most often, which were on the top row, was almost twice as much as on the romaji typewriter, which meant that the time taken to get the fingers there was almost twice as much. His test, Ogata considered, dispelled the widespread popular misconception that typing on a romaji typewriter took twice as much time as using a kana machine by showing the difference to be only about 1:1.3, a gap which was further closed by certain infelicities of key disposition in the kana typewriter which meant that in actual typing the speed was about the same (Ogata 1988: 20–23).

Another researcher took the comparison a step further by including the Japanese (ie kanji) typewriter as well. The kanji typewriter needed a trained typist and could achieve a speed of about 53 characters per minute. The same sentence typed in kana could be done at a speed of 60 characters per minute. The kana typewriter required a training period of between six months and a year. Its speed was 250–300 strokes per minute. At an average of five strokes per word, this worked out to be about 50 to 60 words per minute. The western, or romaji, typewriter could be used by any typist with ordinary training, and could produce 450 strokes (the equivalent of about 90 words) per minute. These figures were arrived at in 1959 – in that year, the winner of the world typing contest achieved a speed of 125 words per minute on a western typewriter (Furukawa 1962: 26).

Both the katakana and hiragana typewriters, and of course the romaji typewriter, offered the Japanese the freedom of using a comparatively simple (albeit non-standardised) keyboard rather than the infinitely more complex, bulky and time-consuming tray-and-arm system of the kanji typewriter. Given the flexibility they offered, then, one might think that they would have gained wider acceptance than they did in Japanese offices. If the choice was between the kanji typewriter, with all its attendant problems and need for specialist operators, and the hiragana or kana typewriter which was cheaper, smaller, faster and could be operated by ordinary office staff once trained, the latter might have seemed a reasonable instrument for document production of a business or personal nature. And so it might have been were it not for that one major defect we have already encountered: that text produced on such a machine did not represent the way Japanese was really written and was difficult to read for people accustomed to kanji. The experience of a member of the Asahi Shinbun's editorial staff illustrates this nicely on a personal level. Wishing to avoid both the sight of his own bad handwriting and the physical fatigue which resulted from writing with a pencil, this journalist bought a typewriter which could type only hiragana, numerals and the alphabet. However, what this meant in practice, he found, was that it could only be used for private documents which were not meant to be shown to other people, as the hiragana-only text seemed too strange without kanji. In the end, he gave the machine to his children to play with (Mizoe 1982: 11).

Despite the relatively successful adoption of katakana typewriters in large offices concerned with billing, then, there was a great deal of opposition to their unconditional adoption as the overall basis of office modernisation because of the unacceptable nature of the text they produced. The failure of forty years of effort to produce an acceptable katakana typewriter could not be blamed on any inherent deficiency in katakana itself but on the deep-seated Japanese preference for the mixed script, a preference which is far stronger than katakana supporters like to admit. The primary appeal of kanji is to emotion ahead of reason, and the ordinary person was inclined to think that text written in kanji had deeper significance and carried more weight than kana text (Miyabara, Takeuchi et al. 1968: 24). It was this deepseated emotional appeal of kanji which led to the impasse in office document production and thence eventually to the rapid development of alternative reproduction and transmission technologies such as the fax and the photocopier which could expedite the circulation and delivery of handwritten documents in the absence of a satisfactory typewriter.

Despite the development of compensatory technologies of this kind, however, the lack of any machine which could produce printed Japanese text at an acceptable speed within acceptable time limits remained a stumbling block to effective office automation in Japan. Opponents of kanji, of course, continued to highlight this to support their contention that only if Japan were to abolish characters could the typewriter be used successfully. In the event, however, they were to be defeated by the leap from mechanical to electronic document production which was just around the corner as office automation finally took root in Japan.

Office automation

There were several factors pointing to the desirability of office automation in general. One was an overall increase in the number of staff employed in the companies' business management divisions; this led to a need to decrease personnel expenses and increase work efficiency. Computers had been used in the early stages to manage large volumes of standard numerical information. By contrast, office work was non-standard and fragmented in nature, and was perceived as likely to benefit from automation. At the same time, computers were becoming smaller, cheaper and easier to use, so that it became possible for medium and small businesses, which until then had done work by hand or sent it out to subcontractors, to acquire them. Large companies could also then handle small-scale specialised office work in each of their sections (rather than having all the work sent to one section for handling). A big breakthrough occurred when the technology advanced to the point of being able to handle documents as well as just figures; numerical information accounted for only about 30% of the documentation in office work, the rest being text and images. And finally, in an age of change, companies needed time freed up to concentrate on creative and comprehensive business decisions and sales activities without wasting it on information handling and document production (Kitahara and Aoki 1982: 230–231).

The differences in office automation between the United States and Japan were threefold. Firstly, and most obviously, the language difference: whereas with the alphabet the word processor was a natural progression from the typewriter, in Japan office automation could not proceed until a way was found to manage kanji. Secondly, there were differences in organisation and organisational climate. In the United States, clear job differentiation had resulted in specialisation; because job descriptions were clear, the effect that the introduction of machines would have on individuals was also clear, leading to resistance to the implementation of office automation. In Japan, on the other hand, with the lifelong employment system and system of rotation between jobs, job descriptions were not so sharply differentiated. This meant that the impact of office automation could be absorbed more easily and thus that there was little resistance to the idea. Finally, there were differences in the flow of office work. In the United States, management first took decisions and the work then flowed down to lower levels. In Japan, where bottom-up decision-making through consultative procedures was the norm, informal information carried considerable weight, necessitating the production and transmission of documents in the process. It was therefore a top priority in Japan to develop a machine that could be used easily by everyone (Kitahara and Aoki 1982: 232–233).

Office automation meant various things to various people, not all of them purely instrumental. In the early 1960s, it was often seen in terms of national pride. Japan had made remarkable strides in the fields of mining, manufacturing and agriculture and as a result its economy had grown rapidly. These fields, however, were concerned with the production of *things*. The one area in which Japan was not fulfilling its economic potential was in its offices. It was felt that office efficiency needed to be raised to the level of the advanced countries of the west if Japan were to take its place in the world as an advanced industrial nation (Furukawa 1962: 11). Twenty years later, office automation (OA) was perceived in terms of a response to the much more advanced factory automation (FA), in which it was already possible to find factories without human operators. The term 'office automation' itself took in the office environment, organisation, the way in which work was done, and the machines that helped do it. Reasons advanced for why businesses were working hard to achieve OA included the increase in and ageing of office populations, the influx of information, and the rapid development of computer technology (Kaji 1982: 84).

The two most immediately apparent environmental factors in modern business that led to office automation were of course the economic factor and the technological revolution factor. The former worked thus: after the oil shock, economic growth went into a slump. Business could no longer make economies of scale, products and services became fragmented, and as a result there was an increase in associated office work. However, because offices were not yet automated, most of this work had to be done by hand. Although office staff were perceived as working hard, inability to save time in office procedures hampered office productivity. The second factor was the speed of the technological revolution, centring around electronics technology, most of which was concerned with areas of information processing and communication. The business activities of a firm could be impeded if the collection, use and management of information in its offices was not done properly. Although many companies had a section designated the 'office work' section, in fact office activity went on in all departments (purchasing, production control, sales, personnel, to name but a few); what was common to them all was the creation, handling, storing and transmission of information (Suzuki 1984: 19–20).

Clearly, something needed to be done about Japan's progress in this area. Moritani (1982: 199–200), summed up the situation:

> While Japan leads the world in industrial productivity, it still lags far behind the United States in the office ... The office is the final frontier for rationalisation. In a sense, it is only natural that the productivity of 'intellectual production' in the office has not increased the same way as has physical production productivity in the factory. Mechanisation has been slow in coming; the ratio of physical investment per worker is less than one-tenth of

> that for factories. In other words, companies spend only one-tenth as much money per office worker as they do for workers in plants and factories. Japan is particularly behind the times in this respect, with the total investment per white-collar worker averaging between $900 and $1400 ... In fact, conditions in the office are still in a pre-industrial-revolution state compared with the industrial sector. This is why so many people in Japan have begun to speak of an 'industrial revolution' in intellectual production.

Moritani went on to speak of the increased ability of computers to handle more than just calculations of numerical data as the trigger for the office revolution and forecast that the key weapon in that revolution would be the Japanese word processor. At the time at which he wrote, this prediction was just beginning to come true.

Romanisation: a serious alternative?

It is worthwhile taking a short detour here, before we go on with the discussion of the new technology, to consider whether romanisation would ever really have been a viable option in solving the office automation dilemma. There were two options for overcoming the input-output difficulty with typewriters: either come up with a technology which would deal more successfully with the problem, or get rid of the source of the problem by abolishing characters. As we have seen, this second alternative did seem more attractive to some, who concluded that Japan would be better off adopting the western alphabet. Such calls for romanisation were not new; there had been small lobby groups advocating such a move since the Meiji period (1867–1911) on the grounds of educational efficiency. In the era of internationalisation and increasing globalisation of many aspects of life, the modern argument ran, would it not make perfect sense for Japan, noted for its history of adaptation, to adapt to the demands of the computer age by jettisoning its troublesome orthography and accepting the Western 'common sense' hegemony of romanisation? A few, such as well-known scholar Yamada Hisao, former director of the research and development department of the National Centre for Science Information Systems, mentioned earlier in this chapter, have argued strongly in favour of romanisation, believing that the new information era requires language which is simple to read and write and that characters do not meet these needs (Yamada 1984: 10–14).

But the use of characters has continued, in fact shows no likelihood of ever ending, and of course it is not merely cultural values relative to script which have been responsible for this. Infrastructure considerations have also played a major, indeed the deciding, role, not that the question has ever really been seriously considered. Structuralist political scientist Steven Reed warns against what he terms the 'fundamental attribution error', in which 'in analysing other nations we tend to overestimate differences in values and underestimate differences in situations. We need to pay less attention to the way the Japanese think and more attention to the context of their behaviour, the circumstances to which they are reacting' (1993: 25). Applied to the romanisation issue, this argument reminds us that we ought not to overrate the importance of cultural mindsets on script relative to the overriding consequence of the prevailing structural environment. The *situation* regarding script in Japan, the practical mechanics of the existing printing and educational infrastructure, is of equal if not greater importance in determining decisions on the issue. Reed warns against underestimating the influence of the environment and overemphasising 'inside-of-the-head variables' (31). It is important here to resist the temptation to construct a culturalist argument which constitutes Japan's success in developing word processing technology as its way of fighting off the threat of cultural imperialism represented by romanisation. In reality, the development of this technology never really signalled the end of a choice between romanisation and characters at all, because romanisation was never seen as a viable option by the majority of Japanese. Given the combined weight of the cultural and political marginalisation of its advocates and the existing character-oriented infrastructure, the choice was always going to be simply one between printed and handwritten documents.

The issue of cultural heritage, of course, as opposed to cultural values, would have been an important factor in rejecting any serious consideration of romanisation. Novelist Endō Shūsaku (1923–1996) grappled in his works with the problem of whether or not Japan can profitably import western cultural products, in his case Christianity, without the accompanying cultural baggage inappropriate to the Japanese context. In the case of the Japanese script, the jettisoning of characters in favour of the alphabet, which opponents would have seen as the ultimate form of cultural imperialism, would have been important not only in terms of the imposition of symbolic foreign anglo-centrist orthographic values but also in terms of an abrupt discontinuity between the future and the accumulated literary values, cutting Japan off from centuries of its own literary heritage. It was the cultural baggage of Japan itself which would have been in question. Over time, the literary corpus of the past could have been rewritten in romaji, of course, but those wishing to read the great literature of the past as it was originally written or to do research using pre-romanisation documents would have been faced with the same task of learning script which faces non-Japanese today.

The barriers to romanisation were therefore threefold: the perception of orthographic self-sufficiency in the modernisation stakes, the entrenched existing character-oriented social infrastructure and the cultural heritage argument. In any case, the development in Japan of technology enabling rapid character retrieval in the late 1970s put paid to any remaining hopes of romanisation by solving the hitherto stubborn input-output problem, although in the area of computer-based communication in particular some argue for it still (Unger 1987, Yamada 1994, Hannas 1997). In 1978 Toshiba announced that it was working on a word processor designed specifically for the Japanese language, with a keyboard of forty-six kana keys and a conversion system which entailed the user pressing a button to have the kana which had been input converted into Chinese characters brought from storage in memory. To go back to our example sentence: to type this on a word processor is much faster and simpler than on a Japanese typewriter (although still not as fast as if the typing were done in English or romanised Japanese). The text can be typed in in either hiragana or romaji which are automatically converted to hiragana, and then converted to the correct character equivalents where necessary simply by pressing the conversion key (called the *kana-kanji henkan* key) (see Lunde 1993 for technical details). Sometimes a character which has the same reading but a different meaning is displayed, in which case it is necessary to keep pressing the key until the right one appears. This can be done easily on the screen as many times as necessary before the document is printed out, whereas with a typewriter, with its instant output, a mistake results in having to redo the document. The invention of Japanese word processing technology was therefore clearly a major breakthrough in machine production of documents, and the next chapter will examine the circumstances of its development in detail. Before we proceed with that, however, let us pause for a moment to consider briefly some of the consequences of the technology for life in Japan which later chapters will develop more fully.

Implications of the technology: a local reading

The local implications of this technology are many and varied. On a first, most obvious level, it has of course enabled Japan to make strides in office automation, as we have already discussed. Passin notes that the Japanese understanding of the word 'internationalisation' in the 1980s included an element of maintaining parity with other advanced industrial societies: 'related is the concept of being competitive, being up-to-date, being up on the latest state-of-the-art technology' (1983: 21). The new technology satisfied the demands of pride in this respect by enabling Japan to catch up with the west on the office automation front while at the same time preserving its own orthography, thereby also meeting the needs of the local environment.

Then there is the status of the word processor within the consumer profile of an increasingly technology-literate society. Once the price of the early word processor dropped to within the grasp of the average person, the *waapuro* became one of the 1980s icons of the culture of consumerism in Japan, reinforcing the image of Japanese as avid consumers of the new. In a sense this technology is a good example of Japan's metaphorical 'consumption' of the west, building on western technological breakthroughs in the field and reshaping them to fit Japan's own needs, as has been the pattern throughout its recorded history. In the more concrete sense of consumerism, its wildfire spread among the population certainly exemplifies the middle-class consumer society par excellence which modern Japan has become, in which 'the mark of an individual is his purchases and possessions' (Miyoshi 1989: 156). In the late 1980s, newspaper paragraphs reported instances of perfectly functioning word processors relegated to rubbish collection heaps solely because they had been replaced by their owners with the latest model.

In terms of techno-paradigm shifts, the appearance of the word processor is an example of successful demand articulation in technology development in Japan, where demand articulation is defined as 'a dynamic interaction of technological activities that involve integrating potential demands into a product concept and decomposing this concept into development agendas for its individual component technologies' (Kodama 1991: 80). In the case of Japanese word processors, described as an illustration of the process of integrating potential demands into a product concept, demand articulation was made possible by careful investigations into a cultural factor, namely the bottleneck in office automation being caused by inadequate typewriters because of the nature of the Japanese script. (Note that while script as a cultural factor is seen as causing the bottleneck, no consideration is given to changing the cultural and social infrastructure on that account.) The kanji-capable word processor is therefore a good example of the demarcation between the local and the global in collective technology research. Kodama postulates a taxonomy of economic incentives for rival firms to participate in collective research, dividing the whole into science projects, whose aim is the collection of scientific knowledge in the 'public good', and technology, where the objective is to arrive at technical breakthroughs with commercial applications. Most international collective projects, he notes, are scientific projects, whereas 'the majority of collective research on technology developments is conducted within national borders' (93). The history of the collective research which resulted in the word processor in Japan exemplifies this contention.

In the literary and social arenas, the appearance of the word processor has also signalled the beginning of a profound change in the way in which Japanese writers engage with text production in the intellectual as well as the mechanical sense of the term. Whereas the function of the typewriter is simply to produce clean copy, the word processor can be used at all stages of the writing process, from the rough notes stage through all intermediate stages to the final product. This capacity contributes to the view of the word processor not just as a typewriter which can handle characters but as a powerful tool for intellectual production. Features such as editing functions, memory and multi-copy printing make the electronic word processor perfectly suited to the actual writing of manuscripts on-screen as opposed to the mere reproduction of already-composed manuscripts on a typewriter based on mechanical principles. Using word processors is seen as a means of freeing up time for true creativity in language classes in schools, particularly at middle and high school levels, by removing the need to spend so much time on memorising characters. Until now, the argument runs, essay writing classes have really just been spent on practice in writing characters. Now that word processors have done away with the need to spend hours learning how to write kanji, students will be able to concentrate instead on learning how to write well, and to focus on content rather than form.

A common view expressed in early twentieth-century perspectives on the Meiji Period injection of western technology into Japan is that it brought about a disjunction between progress and culture. 'From this early perspective, technological progress, the measurable improvement of efficient production, was determined to be a different order of things from aesthetic and cultural forms, for these latter did not (and ought not to be allowed to) change' (Najita 1989: 10). It is certainly true, as we have seen, that in the area of document production technology and orthographic culture came into collision, with the latter hampering the former and new fax technology being developed to compensate for this. Electronic character retrieval, however, has diminished the gap so that advanced technology, in this case certainly a 'measurable improvement of efficient production', and long-standing cultural values sit comfortably together with functionality accountable to indigenous practice.

Of course, in considering the implications of this new technology for Japanese society, we must do more than look only at the kind of instrumental advantages just outlined. Any new technology brings in its wake cultural consequences for the society which adopts it, and the word processor is no exception. In order to arrive at an understanding of the significance of these developments, we must go beyond the immediately apparent and ask ourselves, what of the users of that technology themselves? What sort of effect on Japanese society is produced by the decision, say, to use a word processor rather than a pen (or even a brush) in personal communications? There are two aspects to consider here: the orthographic consequences which, taken together over time, may impact on the larger social issue of national script policy, and the cumulative social consequences of personal choices taken to write with a machine rather than by hand. As to the former, the earlier constraints on the capacity of the writer to remember and to use large numbers of characters have now been lifted, although those on the capacity of the reader to recognise have not. It has, however, always been the norm to be able to recognise more than one can reproduce – the real hardship in handwriting lies in the difficulty of remembering to write a large character set correctly. This was one of the underlying arguments for the postwar script reforms which saw limits placed on the number of characters to be taught in schools for general use. The newspapers also, for fifty years prior to those reforms, had been vocal advocates of character limits for reasons of production economy and circulation during the era of movable type. The adoption of the new word processing technology by the press and the spread of its use in society at large therefore implies that a major plank supporting the Japanese government's present policy on script has now been removed, as we shall see in Chapter Three.

On the second count, one might expect that the proliferation of more impersonal printed documents would create a greater feeling of social distance between writer and reader. To the extent that this is so, the technology could be seen as having a transformative agency in areas of social intercourse. How does the use of word processing affect habits and values? Are older habits and values being replaced with new ones or merely modified, and to what extent have those changes acquired social significance? While many people view this technology as a means for enhancing communication, others see it as converting one aesthetically and morally prized means of written communication into something inferior. But does this argument carry any weight with younger people brought up surrounded by electronic devices? In this sense the old values relative to forms of reading and writing are undergoing change, and to use a word processor signals a particular view of one's stance in this particular social debate. We will consider these issues at length in Chapter Four. First, however, let us see just how the new technology made its appearance on the scene and what its reception was.

CHAPTER TWO

Early Days

It was against the background described in Chapter One that, late in 1978, the first Japanese word processor capable of handling all three scripts through a process of electronic conversion from kana input to kanji output appeared. This was the Toshiba JW-10, a stand-alone machine (ie not a personal computer using word processing software) which was put on show at a trade fair in Tokyo that year. It was marketed as being a document production and editing machine for businesses, with functions accordingly slanted in that direction. The cost was 6.3 million yen, and the machine weighed 220 kilograms.

What the Toshiba machine could do that the Japanese typewriter could not was store many thousands of characters in its internal memory, allow input through a kana or romaji keyboard, and permit editing of documents on screen before a final printing. No longer was it necessary to search for one character among several thousand in the bulky trays of the traditional typewriter. Instead, the operator could type in the word in kana and then press the conversion button to bring the kanji for that word up from the internal dictionary on to the screen. Where there was more than one possibility, the correct one could be selected from the alternatives on offer. Once the text was input to the satisfaction of the operator, it could then be edited, parts deleted, other parts added, all done on the screen without printing out. As editing a document produced by a typewriter meant that editing was done on paper and any changes made, no matter how small, would necessitate a retyping of the entire document, this promised no small saving of time. The final stage was printing, after all changes had been satisfactorily made. Documents could be stored on disk and recalled at any time for printing or for other use.

The official 1,945-character List of Characters for General Use, drawn up under the aegis of the Education Ministry, forms the basis of national script policy. The much greater number of kanji stored within a word processor, however, was decided not by the Education Ministry but by the Ministry of International Trade and Industry (MITI), which in 1978 issued the first Japan Industrial Standards (JIS) list of computer codes for characters. This list was revised in 1983. The characters, 6,353 in total, were set out in two levels, decided on the basis of frequency of use. Level One contained 2,965 basic characters that were estimated to be of very high frequency in business documents, in addition to hiragana, katakana, numerals, symbols, the roman alphabet and the Greek alphabet. The 3,390 characters in Level Two were not used every day but occurred in personal or place names or in certain specialised genres of scholarly writing. At first, some cheap word processors included only Level One, as more than 99% of ordinary writing could be covered with these characters; however, it was not long before Level Two was included as well. In 1990, in response to requests from the printing industry and complaints from those who worked in specialised fields and could not find certain characters they needed in the first two levels, MITI announced a third set of 5,801 characters known as the JIS supplementary *kanji*, bringing the total number to 12,156 (Atsuji 1991: 219–220). These supplementary characters are not contained in word processors; they still contain only the JIS Levels One and Two, which were further revised in 1990 and 1997, bringing them to a total of 6,355. The revisions consisted mainly of shifting characters between the two levels rather than adding new ones (Sakamura 1998: 2).

The word processor was therefore much more versatile than the Japanese typewriter, which could only produce clean copy and could not easily handle revisions; it could be used from the first-draft stage through the editing process to the final production, and could also store information. In 1983, the four main functions of the new machine were summarised as: keying in a document (input), on-screen editing, printing the document (output) and storage and retrieval. A survey conducted to find out which of the four functions people found most convenient found that 8% of respondents nominated input, 51% editing, 6% printing and 33% storing on disk. In other words, as we might expect, the two functions not found on the typewriter were those most appreciated on the word processor. The surprisingly low figures for input and printing probably indicated some dissatisfaction with the input and output functions, ie there could be a simpler way to input Japanese text and print quality needed improving. Not all word processors in 1983 used today's universal kana-kanji conversion method of inputting characters; the variety of input methods then available resulted in a variety of speeds. Sharp's pen-touch method, for example, where the characters were all laid out as they had been on a kanji typewriter and were selected with a pen, allowed approximately fifty characters per minute; Toshiba's kana-kanji conversion around sixty to eighty; and Hitachi's two-stroke method (which used a JIS-layout hiragana keyboard but converted characters one by one, thereby necessitating two strokes) in theory could allow an ordinary user to reach about 100 characters per minute once the method was mastered to the point of automaticity (Itō 1983: 61–62).

The seemingly revolutionary nature of the potential application of the new technology of course attracted comment, usually in comparative terms with the west as exemplar. In the USA, the development of the word processor was no more than a process of continuation, building first on the mechanical typewriter and later on the electric typewriter. In Japan, however, it represented a major revolution in office practice, heralding a shift from the 'clean copy only' capabilities of the typewriter to a machine which could be used for real writing rather than mere reproduction. Because Japan had been able to take advantage of the recent advances in mechatronics, one commentator noted, it had done in five years what it had taken the west 150 years to do, without the advantage of having gone through its own typewriter stage. Nevertheless, despite the rapid adoption of the new technology, it would take many years of experimentation and experience to fully acculturate the technology to the same degree as other countries by now had, so that it only seemed on the surface as if Japan had caught up (Tatsuoka 1984: 5–6).

The development of the Japanese word processor was indeed made possible by rapid advancements in computer technology over the preceding years, thus supporting the view that all technological development is an evolutionary rather than revolutionary process. Added to this general advance in the field was the specific improvement in kanji input, fuelled by the desire to be able use Japanese-language input rather than just numerical input, romaji or katakana, or English-language computer languages such as Fortran and Cobol. The kana-kanji conversion process on the word processor was of course underpinned by computer technology. Toshiba's Mori Ken'ichi, who had developed the new machine, listed as further triggers for its appearance the first computerisation boom in newspapers, which led to the idea that the production process could be hastened if computers could be used at the editing stage, and the telex machine – the telex printed in katakana and romaji and communications came from overseas in both romanised Japanese and in English, both of which were difficult to read. Any new machine developed to meet these needs had to possess three essential attributes: it must be a tool which could type Japanese faster than handwriting; it must be portable, so that it could be taken anywhere rather than being restricted to a designated word processing room; and it must have a communication function in order to communicate via a telephone line (Mori, Yamane et al. 1988: 6). This was in fact what developed over the first ten years of the word processor's existence, with the most difficult to achieve being the solving of the input problem.

The idea for Toshiba's JW-10 had come from the technical team of the Mainichi newspaper. A joint development project between the Mainichi and Toshiba had started seven years earlier in 1971, centred on the development of a high-speed *kantere* (kanji telex) system to satisfy the demand for faster communication between the Mainichi's main office in Tokyo and the regional bureaux. The *kantere* was the predecessor of the word processor in the newspaper room. It was a heavy machine weighing several hundred kilos, which required a specially trained operator to key in the news items in a very complex system requiring the manipulation of two foot pedals in one of four ways in order to input the required character from one of approximately 600 keys. What the Mainichi wanted to do was develop a machine that journalists themselves could use rather than having to rely on an operator to punch in the articles, thereby improving productivity by opening up new skills in a larger sector of its workforce. As things stood, not only could journalists not operate the *kantere*, it was also too big to fit on their desks. The development team therefore began brainstorming to come up with a new machine which did not require any real training and was portable.

Mori's concept for a new product which would satisfy the requirement of newspaper production was encapsulated in the three essential attributes described above. The speed of input was particularly important: at 50–70 characters per minute, the *kantere* was faster than the Japanese typewriter's 30 characters per minute, but still lagged behind handwriting at 70 characters per minute. Mori originally thought in terms of improving the *kantere*, developing the idea of designing a keyboard that would accommodate the Japanese script so that anyone could use it. The keyboard, however, which required operation with the tip of a pen, at 60 characters per minute, still did not reach the same speed as handwriting or the *kantere* itself. Mori therefore abandoned the idea of improving the telex and directed his attention to developing a system whereby kana input would be automatically converted to kanji where required by a system which matched up kana with characters stored in an internal electronic dictionary. Some work on this idea had already been done by Kurihara Toshihiko of Kyushu University in 1964. The Kyōdō Tsūshin press agency and NHK, the national broadcaster, were also experimenting with systems whereby news cables written in the alphabet and sent by telex by foreign correspondents could be converted into kana and kanji in Japan, but both trials had proved unsatisfactory. The biggest problem was how to correctly convert the large number of homophones in Japanese.

Mori himself attempted to read widely on the fundamentals of Japanese grammar and lexicon, but was told by specialists in these areas that there was little research in his areas of interest, the reason being that language was in a constant state of flux and immutable laws were thin on the ground. This, of course, was not what he needed to hear – language may indeed be imprecise, but a machine needs precise instructions to follow. A grammar-based system was clearly not possible, Mori concluded, but it would be important to have each and every word recorded in the internal dictionary. To decide on where to cut kana input for conversion, the team adopted the Hashimoto grammar method used in schools which was based on the premise that sentences are strings of syntactic units (*bunsetsu*). In principle, *bunsetsu* are constructed of free forms (independent words such as nouns, verbs and adjectives) and bound forms such as particles and auxiliary verbs. The computer looked for independent words first, which often led to parts of what was in fact a verb being converted into a noun, eg the 'ha' of the verb 'hashiranai' (not run) would be offered as 'tooth' or 'leaf', both also pronounced 'ha'. This method was adopted in late 1974, but was still not the full answer: the success rate for correct conversion continued to hover around 70%.

The root cause of the mistaken conversions, those that gave the wrong kanji for the context, was narrowed down through painstaking experiment to the homophones that make up a large part of the Japanese lexicon. In even a small dictionary, with fewer than 60,000 entries, over 35% of the entries will be homophones (Yamada 1984: 8). The word 'kōshō', for example, could have upwards of twenty different meanings: how was the word processor dictionary to know, when the word was input in kana from the keyboard, that it was the characters meaning 'refined' which were required in one instance and those meaning 'negotiations' in another? In order to increase the successful conversion rate to over 90%, Mori looked at including in the word processor a 'learning' function. The short-term version of this operates on the basis that if the word 'negotiation' appears once in a document there is a high probability that it will be used again. When that word is input again, therefore, the kanji meaning 'negotiation' are offered first when the conversion key is pressed. The long-term version is the one in which the homophones most often used come earlier in the list and those seldom used are further down the line, ie rather than having to sift through the various versions of 'kōshō' to arrive at the correct one, those most likely to be required come up first. Using both these short- and long-term learning functions, Mori was able to achieve his target rate of 95% correct conversions (Tanaka 1991: 29–37).

The matter of the potential market for the new machine exercised the minds of profit-oriented Toshiba executives and led to some strong opposition to its development within the company. Would such a machine sell in numbers sufficient to justify its production expenses? In 1978, the strongest opponent was the head of Toshiba's operations division, on the grounds of where to focus the potential market. There were at the time around 100,000 specialist typists using the Japanese typewriter. The division head thought the market should be restricted to these people, and was sceptical of claims that the kana-kanji conversion process would enable typing that was faster than writing by hand and needed little training. In the end, he proposed a test: if a young woman from the company's general affairs section with no previous typing experience could type a document more quickly than he himself could make a clean copy by hand, he would be convinced. Mori accordingly borrowed a young woman, sent her to typing school for two months to train on a kana typewriter, and on the last day taught her about the function keys of the word processor. The idea was that she would thus be enabled to input the entire text quickly in kana and then do the kanji conversions at the end. On the appointed day, the division head timed her with a stopwatch, was persuaded by the results, and gave his imprimatur for the Toshiba JW-10 to be displayed at the upcoming trade fair (Mori, Yamane et al. 1988: 7–9).

Once the Toshiba machine was on the market, it was not long before other companies followed. Sharp, Brother, Canon and Fujitsu, among others, all produced word processors over the next few years. First on the scene after Toshiba was Sharp in 1979 with the Shoin WD-3000, at a cost of 2,950,000 yen; then in 1980 came Fujitsu's Oasys 100 (2,700,000 yen), Canon's Kyanowaado 55 (2,600,000 yen), Toshiba's JW-10 Model 2 (3,400,000 yen), NEC's NWP-20N (4,250,000 yen) and Matsushita's JD-1000 (2,880,000 yen). The following year saw a flurry of nineteen different models (Atsuji 1991: 151).

Most of these early versions did not offer a keyboard kana-kanji conversion type of input, which takes many years of research to develop, but used the previously mentioned 'pen-touch' or 'tablet' method of input, where the characters were all laid out in a large matrix and were selected with the touch of a pen. The pen-touch method was originally thought to be easiest for Japanese typists, who were envisaged as the main users and were accustomed to this layout. Mori's team had earlier trialed it but had rejected it on the basis of poor results. Their tests showed that whereas the input speed of the kana-kanji conversion method was 50 to 100 characters per minute, that of the pen-touch method, even for a trained operator, was only 30 to 50 (Mori 1980: 8). There was also a belief that writing by hand would be faster and that ordinary people (ie not trained specialist typists) would find it too difficult to remember the arrangement of the keys. Toshiba's competitors adopted this input method because they hoped business users would more easily accept it. Sales were bad, however, and after about 1982 they changed to kana-kanji conversion with a keyboard. Sharp's Terakawa Kazunobu lamented later that he would not have believed that the so-called 'keyboard allergy' of the Japanese people could disappear as quickly as it did (Tanaka 1991: 42).

Another who was instrumental in the early development of the word processor was Fujitsu's Kanda Yasunori. Fujitsu followed its very expensive 1980 Oasys with the much cheaper My Oasys in 1982, thus opening the way for the mass spread of the word processor. In the early part of his career as a hardware engineer with Fujitsu, Kanda had spent much time attempting to catch up to the IBM computers. It seemed to him that the Japanese had simply taken over a computer which the Americans, who spoke English, had designed for their own use. This did not particularly matter as long as only mathematical knowledge was required, as a differential equation looked the same regardless of language. Once language was involved, however, computers would be of limited use in Japan unless some way could be found to handle Japanese script electronically. It was imperative that the keyboard, as the point of interface between user and machine, be useable by ordinary people and not just trained operators (Kanda 1984: 85).

On a television program in May 1982, Kanda raised eyebrows by predicting that word processor sales would reach ten million. Others on the same program had made more conservative estimates: the Sharp representative, for instance, had cited a figure of half a million, and the Toshiba person five million. Kanda's prediction was based on the fact that of Japan's estimated 40 million workers, approximately ten million worked at desks in offices (Tanaka 1991: 46). The early machines were very definitely designed with business users as their primary target. Nakamura Shōzaburō, who worked on developing the first Japanese front-end processor (Matsutake), confirmed that the policy of his organisation was to shape both the kanji conversion process and the contents of the internal dictionary to fit the needs of the business user. It was felt that the exorbitant price of the machines at the time would preclude ownership by individuals and would mean that word processors would be used by small to medium businesses and in the different departments of large firms. The dictionaries therefore targeted for inclusion those words most likely to be used in business documents. This was also the policy of the company which developed the VJE front-end processor: because they feared that the limited capacity of floppy disks would not allow an entire Japanese language dictionary to be entered, they first weeded out those words unlikely to be used in an office context (Hagiwara, Nakamura et al. 1988: 10–12).

Some early case studies

How successful were the developers in meeting the needs of their business consumers? A survey of early word processor use carried out by the Japan Association for the Development of Information Processing in 1981 included case studies of the experiences of companies which had decided to incorporate word processors into their offices. These accounts provide us with interesting information on the expectations with which companies approached the purchase of the new technology and the extent to which those expectations were met.

Adachi Hiroshi, of Sony's computer division, reported on his company's experiences with the Toshiba JW-10, which was introduced into the general affairs section with the aim of reducing the work needed for typing, thus achieving savings in both labour and personnel. At the time the report was written, one full-time operator working almost all day long on the JW-10 was able to produce in one month about one thousand pages of printed documents. There had also been personnel savings in that the company now employed two fewer Japanese typists than before. However, of the work produced, about 80% involved the creation of new documents; those things which the word processor was reputed to be good for, ie editing and processing retrieved documents, accounted for only 20%. At that stage, the company reported, the JW-10 was being used mainly as a clean-copy machine, just like the Japanese typewriter, with frequent requests for clean copy coming from other sections in the company. This indicated that there was insufficient understanding within the company of the functions of the word processor, which needed to be actively promoted to increase awareness.

The machine was being used at Sony for such jobs as production of circulars, regulations, minutes of meetings, contracts, manuals, and databases of addresses. While the general affairs section found itself unable as yet to reduce the number of its Japanese typewriters, due to the volume of business, the plan was in future to replace them with word processors. It was not yet possible to shift all the jobs done on the typewriter to the word processor because many people still preferred the appearance of the printed characters produced by the typewriter. Also, the type of paper on which a word processor could print was still limited – it could not, for example, effectively handle the kind of rice paper used for special purposes. Nor was the speed of document production as yet all that remarkably faster than the Japanese typewriter. And finally, there was the price factor – a Japanese typewriter cost 250,000–300,000 yen, compared to two to four million yen for a word processor (Nihon Jōhō Shori Kaihatsu Kyōkai 1981: 53–59).

Reflecting on the company's overall experience, Adachi classified the two broad functions of the word processor as document production (editing and revision functions) and document saving and management. A good balance between the two was important, but there was as yet no word processor on the market which was equally good for both, meaning that a company had to choose the machine which best handled the aspect most important to it. With regard to document production, most of the tasks his company wanted the word processor to do had until then been performed by human beings in the office. Female clerks or secretaries would write the text or make a clean copy of someone else's; the person in charge would look at it and make changes in red; the female clerk would again produce a clean copy. Depending on the time available for the completion of the particular task, this process could be repeated many times over. Handwritten operations were therefore very costly in terms of time and layout, and it was rare that the revisions ended up being perfect. Unless the document in question was a very important one, some compromise short of perfection would usually ensue. The editing functions of the word processor, however, bypassed this process, particularly in view of the fact that the same stored document could be retrieved and used with appropriate editing as many times as was necessary. The machine was therefore good for document production, but needed more work before it could successfully handle the file management tasks.

The word processor had two other advantages apart from its editing and storage functions. One was that it made writing kanji easy – so long as the user knew the pronunciation of the word, in order to input it in either kana or romaji, the machine would supply the kanji which the user might very well have forgotten exactly how to write. When one took into account that people could usually read more kanji than they could write by hand, this was a very useful function, which resulted not only in an increase in the number of kanji a person could use but in greater accuracy than handwriting in the text. The other was that the user could see straight away what he or she had written in printed form, whereas with handwriting it was quite difficult for amateurs to visualise what their handwritten manuscripts would look like when printed.

Adachi had a few cautionary observations to offer. One was to avoid word processors equipped with the pen-touch input method rather than the kana-kanji conversion. As in the case of the Japanese typewriter on which it was modelled, touch typing was impossible with this method because of the need to confirm each character visually before touching it with the pen. Another related to the operators: the former specialist typists naturally felt vaguely uneasy about the new machine, not just about its novelty, which could be overcome with training, but about the possible loss of future income if they should want to continue as part-time typists after they left work and took up domestic duties. They feared that if they became accustomed to these new machines, which could be used only at the office, they might lose their existing skills as operators of the Japanese typewriter and become slower. To a professional typist, the speed of document production was everything. Office managers should therefore bear this possible staff resistance in mind when introducing word processors to an office where there were already Japanese typists (Nihon Jōhō Shori Kaihatsu Kyōkai 1981: 62–65). Personnel issues at Sony on the one hand were therefore balanced against a degree of increased efficiency, with development of further refinements and more education in the proper use of the machines to their fullest capacity clearly needed.

A second company case study came from Bishika Shisutemu, the information processing company mentioned in Chapter One as being part of Mitsubishi Chemicals. The first condition this company placed on the acquisition of word processors was that they had to be easy to operate and not need a specialist operator. The company also valued intangible savings such as easier to read and better formatted documents, speed of production, and of course the ability to reuse and edit saved documents. The original plan was that the female staff members in each of the company's groups would create the clean copy of the documents produced in that group on the word processor. Two of the female staff were chosen; an instructor from Sharp spent half a day teaching them the machine's functions; these women were then made responsible for teaching the others and for liaising with Sharp about any questions which arose. After the machines were introduced, female staff practised on them for four hours a day. Most people were able to create clean copies of simple letters and similar documents after one or two hours' practice.

This company decided against adopting the western system of allocating typing to certain staff members only and planned instead that all female staff members would be able to use the word processor, in what is called the 'open style' of use. Accordingly, the floppy disks containing documents would be kept and handled by the female staff member on duty in each section. All new staff members were given simple basic instruction as part of their induction process in the operations section; further instruction in the actual business of producing clean copy was done by more experienced members in the section. It was initially intended to use the machines for contracts, as a recent increase in business had led to an increase in the number of contracts needed. There was, of course, a standard contract form, but it usually needed partial modifications to fit particular cases, so although most of the content was the same the company had had no choice but to send each contract out to a typing subcontractor to have the changes made. With a word processor, the standard form could be kept on disk and reformatted through a series of simple steps. For the first six months the machine was used for six hours a day, but at the time of writing that had decreased to about 3.5 hours per day as the female staff became used to it and the number of short editing jobs increased.

Was the machine effective? Yes, was the general verdict. The time taken to make editorial changes to documents had decreased; the speed of operation had increased with practice and familiarity. Also, importantly, because staff no longer had to worry about whether the characters were well or poorly written as with handwriting, both those who requested the clean copy and those who provided it did not suffer any psychological burden. Previously, the main burden of preparing handwritten clean copy had fallen on those whose handwriting was good; people would hesitate to ask those whose handwriting was less good. This problem had now completely disappeared (Nihon Jōhō Shori Kaihatsu Kyōkai 1981: 76–83). In that sense, then, the word processor had no doubt evened out the work load of individuals to some extent, although the task of producing clean copy still rested squarely with the female staff.

One company which adopted, in principle at least, a policy whereby the word processing work would be shared by all, including men and managers, was Eezai. Like the other companies surveyed, this company did not want specialist operators and so looked for a machine to be kept in the general office that could be mastered without special training. In order to ensure that the input method could be easily learned, prior to purchase they tested various makes on male staff members, including managers, who had not previously used Japanese typewriters. As a result, the company decided to purchase a machine with kana-kanji conversion from a hiragana keyboard, rather than one with pen-touch input. During the two-month trial period, the number of documents produced increased to 238, most of which were produced in a short period of time. Good use was made of the editing function as well. The company found that one A4 page, which took 30 minutes on a Japanese typewriter, took 20 minutes by word processor (about the same as handwriting); partial revision of about 180 characters, which still took 30 minutes on the typewriter because the whole document had to be redone, took only seven minutes on the word processor. The original objective of having everyone including managers use it was not achieved; several of the managers did no more than the initial training and none of them were putting it to use, so that at the time the case study was written, only about thirty people, most of them female staff, were using the word processor on a daily basis (Nihon Jōhō Shori Kaihatsu Kyōkai 1981: 84–97). At this stage, the input speed, while faster than the Japanese typewriter, was still only about the same as that of handwriting, owing to difficulty in early models with getting the correct kanji conversions.

By 1983, the word processor had gained more buyer confidence as businesses and government offices began to realise the benefits it could offer. In March that year, 300 companies were surveyed with regard to their office automation practices. When asked what their aim in using office automation was, 43% responded that it was to raise the productivity of office work, bearing out the general perception that the primary objective of OA is to increase efficiency in general office work. Another 23%, however, replied that it was to help individual staff members with information processing and to increase speed and reliability, indicating that OA is not simply concerned with efficiency alone but with assisting the task of information processing and raising the quality of the work. Increasing efficiency involves three things: saving labour, reducing expenditure on office work and speeding up office work by, for example, speeding up the preparation of responses for the Diet by installing car phones in the vehicles of senior executives in the Finance Ministry linked by high speed fax to the Diet. 201 of the 300 companies surveyed answered that office automation had resulted in faster handling of office work. Nor was the trend to using the new machines limited to the private sector: the following year, the Tokyo metropolitan government, where the volume of documents handled in one year was said to equate to a pile twelve times the height of Mt Fuji, announced that it would introduce 110 office machines of different types, including word processors, personal computers, large office computers, faxes and laser disks (Suzuki 1984: 22).

What were the dissemination patterns of the new machines involved in this automation? In 1984, the Saitama Prefectural

Government had six large office computers (called *ofukon* in Japanese, a contraction of the two English words), eleven personal computers and four word processors, with plans to put a fax machine in each section. In business, in the 300 companies looked at in the 1983 survey, each had an average of 2.3 general use computers, 6.4 *ofukon*, 25.9 personal computers, 24.5 faxes, 11.2 word processors and 138.9 on-line terminals. The trend clearly reveals that small machines of a decentralised type which could be used by ordinary staff were quickly spreading in preference to a model in which information processing was centred around large computers.

On the matter of which machines were used to improve which jobs, the survey revealed that the most common was use of office computers and personal computers for a variety of small-scale, personal office work (61%) and entry of information into databases (47%), followed by use of word processors for document production (45%). It was furthermore clear that the companies' general affairs divisions favoured the use of simple, single-use machines (word processors) for text information processing, while the financial and accounting divisions preferred general-use computers for numerical data processing. Office automation was therefore progressing along the path of introducing a variety of different types of machines as appropriate across the whole range of office work, rather than maintaining past dependence on large computers. The survey indicated that OA was on the increase: in 1983 the use of personal computers and word processors had increased to 39.7% from 33.4% the previous year. At the same time, the proportion of text information processing they were used for had increased from 28.1% in 1982 to 33.3% in 1983, indicating that these machines were now being used not just for data processing but also for text production. A comparison of word processor use across different types of division shows that it was quite high in most areas, from 25–45% in most departments, peaking at 61.4% in general affairs divisions and bottoming out at 11.4% among, predictably, top management (Suzuki 1984: 23–27).

Early reactions

At this early stage, despite their manifest advantages, the new machines still had defects. For one thing, they were still very large and could be considered only in the loosest sense portable. Screens in smaller models displayed only one line of text, or at the most half a page. Printers were very noisy, always a problem in an office environment. The kana-kanji conversion process was by no means foolproof. Sometimes, too, the required kanji for personal and place names could not be found in the dictionary. Because each manufacturer had different specifications, there was no compatibility between machines. And they were very, very expensive: smaller machines cost around 1 million yen (or 30–50,000 yen per month to lease), while top of the range models cost 5-6 million yen (or 200,000 yen per month to lease) (Nihon Jōhō Shori Kaihatsu Kyōkai 1981: 98). Many businesses could afford only one, so that where many staff wanted to use it it could be hard to find a time when it was free.

Staff reactions to the introduction of the new machines varied. Early brochures advertising pen-touch word processors promoted them as a way to 'lighten the load' of typists (Mori, Yamane et al. 1988: 8). Nevertheless, Japanese typists, as we have seen, felt predictable concern; they did not want to see their already established skills disappear and they also felt pressured to maintain production efficiency while they were still getting used to the new machine. Nippon Denki's office efficiency promotion section vacillated over whether or not to retrain existing typists as word processor operators and create a class of jobs as specialist operators (a 'closed' system, as opposed to the 'open' system). The word processor was meant to be used by all staff, but from time to time pressure of work might necessitate the services of such specialist operators. The fact that not all word processors had the same type of input system during this early period cast doubt on whether or not such a job description could be created. It was further unclear whether or not in-house use of the word processor saved money compared to outside contracting of typing. Certainly, if a company employee produced a document on a word processor, that involved no outside contractor expenses. On the other hand, as most of the office work had previously been done by hand, such outside expenses were limited to special cases; it was more difficult to pinpoint the personnel expenses involved in in-house production in either the closed or open system of use. In addition to the typists' fears, the same office also reported feelings of disquiet among general office workers who were not used to typing, and who were worried about the length of time it would take them to master the new skill of using a word processor (Nihon Jōhō Shori Kaihatsu Kyōkai 1981: 127–128).

Early resistance on the part of office workers to the idea of using a computer was thus evident in Japan as everywhere else, but it was clear from fairly early on in the 1980s that this would have to be conquered. The writer of the Eezai company case study discussed earlier predicted that the time would soon come when everyone in an office used terminals and keyboards of one kind or another to do their work, and that veteran staff members and managers who suffered from the well known 'computer allergy' would then find themselves unable to function properly (Nihon Jōhō Shori Kaihatsu Kyōkai 1981: 86). Several years later, in 1988, a survey of businesses in Ishikawa prefecture cited the existence of pockets of resistance towards the word processor as one of the hindrances to the spread of word processing skills by 30% of companies which had indicated a wish to proceed further in this direction, along with lack of time on the part of both teacher and learner in about half the companies and lack of motivation on the part of the learner in one third of them (Terai 1988: 161). Three years further on, journalist Tanaka Ryōta confirmed the truth of the Eezai writer's prediction, remarking on the trend among the major newspapers in the 1990s to move towards totally electronic input of news and articles. In the near future, he mused, it might be that nobody would be able to undertake journalistic writing by hand. Journalists who either could not or would not use a word processor would therefore soon be isolated from the whole flow of information constructed in electronic characters (Tanaka 1991: 20). Clearly, in businesses which made the decision to incorporate the new machines, it was imperative to retrain workers and to overcome their resistance in order to reap the maximum benefit.

The likely future of the new technology was variously evaluated in the early days. Toshiba's Kawada Tsutomu thought the word processor would establish itself in offices if the exorbitant cost came down, if it became smaller (to fit on a desk) and later portable, and if the printer's ability to handle envelopes and pre-cut paper improved (Kawada and Amano 1980: 900). Nippon Denki likewise saw it as having good prospects in the business world if the early glitches were fixed, and also as possibly moving into homes for personal use. Overall, however, it is clear that the company saw the word processor only as a clean copy machine: 'whether for office or personal use, the first manuscript will still be handwritten. The longstanding Japanese custom of ordering one's thoughts as one writes by hand will probably not be easily displaced' (Nihon Jōhō Shori Kaihatsu Kyōkai 1981: 133). Not everyone shared that view, which later developments were to prove mistaken. In 1984, another forecast saw users as likely to be semi-professionals and non-professionals, because there would be a shift away from the 'clean copy' function (particularly as new technologies like scanners were introduced) towards a more sophisticated use of the machine for the much more important role of actual writing and composition of text rather than just reproduction. Most machines followed this 'professional to non-professional' trajectory – knowing how to drive the first automobiles, for example, had led to special status jobs for some, but driving was now a skill taken for granted. Similarly, in the west, typing had quickly become a semi-professional rather than professional skill of great use to writers, journalists, public servants and business. This was the path on which the Japanese word processor was seen to be standing poised (Tatsuoka 1984: 4,6).

The Kanamojikai and the Nippon-no-Rōmazi-sya (Japan Romanisation Society) were of course predictably against the new machine because it demolished their main argument, that characters impeded office automation and therefore Japan's progress. A couple of representative comments: Japanese cleverness was to be deplored because commercialisation had as usual brought out the excellence of Japanese technicians (Yamasaki 1982: 23). Using kanji slowed down the speed of typing on a word processor - having to take time to choose between homophones in a sentence, for example. The word processor showed yet again how troublesome and uneconomic the use of kanji was (Ishida 1982: 13). Much to their chagrin, these groups were forced to recognise that the 'chains' of kanji had now been broken in both input and output terms, and that Japan had found its own way to automate document production while still retaining its own script. This did not mean, however, that they lost all hope. Many of the articles appearing in *Kana no Hikari*, the journal of the Kanamojikai, in the 1980s, for example, examined the word processor closely, criticising what they saw as its defects, mostly to do with the high rate of mistaken conversion of homophones, the time needed to correct this which resulted in slower speeds compared to the western word processor and the tendency of the machines to create meaningless compounds owing to misresolution of kana input. Supporters of romanisation likewise wrote a lot about the new technology. Not all were depressed: Muramatsu Shinji, for example, saw the word processor as a golden opportunity for the cause. Romanisation advocates should not reject the word processor too hastily, he cautioned; in fact, the very ease with which its users could retrieve kanji would teach them anew how complex the Japanese script was. In time, users were bound to realise just what a waste of time and energy was involved in learning and using huge numbers of kanji; that would be the perfect opportunity to re-emphasise the ease and practicality of the alphabet. The movement should therefore be looking to revive the romanisation cause with the word processor as its banner (Muramatsu 1985: 52). Muramatsu's argument is still heard sporadically fifteen years later from people convinced that the benefits of romanisation in a computer-centred world outweigh those of retaining the existing writing system, as we shall see in Chapter Five.

A few years later

In 1988, 84 businesses active in Ishikawa prefecture were surveyed in order to discover, ten years after the advent of word processors, how they used them and what their future plans might be. The companies were fairly evenly divided between the manufacturing and non-manufacturing sectors, with an average of 183 employees, and most had introduced word processors either three or five years previously. The three-year mark corresponded to the massive 1985 jump in word processor sales figures, a 150% increase over the previous year, reported in Chapter One. The average number of word processors (which in this survey was taken to include not just dedicated word processors but word processing software used on office and personal computers) in each company was 4.6, with only two companies reporting having none at all.

As might be expected given that word processors are needed for office work, around 90% of the companies reported having staff in the general office who could use them, but many had nobody in other areas who did. The basis for effective word processor use, they said, was not so much knowledge of how to operate the machine itself but an ability to create good documents and a facility with language. Most of their users learned the skill through on the job training, two thirds voluntarily and one third because they were told to. Only 5% of companies offered any special treatment (eg allowances) for word processor users, which indicated that ability to use this machine was by then considered a normal part of the skills required for staff in the general affairs sections of most businesses. Despite a trend in the mid- to late 1980s to send specialist word processor operators to companies on a contract basis or to subcontract document production out, as in the days of the Japanese typewriter, the survey found only one example of this in the companies examined - all the others were using their own staff to do the work.

The work was distributed according to three distinct styles: the closed style, where document handling was entrusted to a designated person who did this either full time or in conjunction with another job; the open style, where everyone used the word processor as needed; and a combination of the two. At the time of the survey, the closed style was used in 37% of companies, compared to the open style in 25%, which indicated that word processing skills were still not as widespread as they might be. When asked how they would prefer to see the machines used, however, 41% of companies responded in favour of the open style, 35% the combination style, and 23% the closed style, ie more people would prefer to do the work themselves than were then doing so. Companies of the size covered by the survey may not have had enough work to use full-time operators (most of those using the closed style reported that their designated operator combined this work with other tasks), outside contractors or visiting temporary operators.

One third (33%) of the companies reported that 'about 75%' of their business documents were now done on word processor. Many reported that documents now looked better and were easier to read, and that filing was easier (others, however, reported no change). Opinion as to whether documents could now be created more quickly than before was fairly evenly divided, with about 15% of respondents replying that it had in fact become slower. Those who cited increased speed attributed this to the ability to create and store standard format documents which could be quickly called up for appropriate changes. One possible reason for the cases of reported slowing down of operations may have been that it takes time to develop the skill of touch-typing and that until it is mastered people have to use the 'hunt and peck' system, which is of course slower than handwriting. In terms of overall effect on the job, however, the most common response was that the quality of the work, regardless of the speed, had improved. 76% indicated that they intended to further spread word processor use within the company, with 69% planning to increase the number of staff who could use one (Terai 1988: 151–162).

A second survey conducted at the ten-year mark in 1988 was carried out by Canon Sales, who contacted 300 male staff between twenty and sixty years of age from listed companies in the Tokyo area in order to determine how 'salarymen' (male office workers) were using word processors. The survey found that word processors had by that time spread into more than 90% of companies, but only 54% of the men surveyed responded that they could use one. 66% of men in their twenties and 41% of those in their fifties were familiar with the machines. One in five of those at the rank of section or division head indicated that they had learned because they had been told to. Only 2% of respondents could touch-type, and only 6% were familiar with and made full use of all functions of the machine. 34% of those who understood basic functions such as inserting and deleting, copying and moving, reported that they seldom used them. One in four people were still writing out a complete draft of their document and then typing it in without change, ie they were using the machine like a typewriter to produce clean copy rather than writing the document on-screen as they went along.

With regard to perceptions of its importance: 15% believed strongly that they would fall behind if they could not use a word processor. One quarter of these people were in their fifties. Overall, 27% of respondents did not believe this would happen. Most reported that the word processor had resulted in improved appearance of documents; other perceived benefits were increased efficiency in work, neater workplaces because documents were filed on disk, and a decrease in the 'bad handwriting complex'. 38% had their own personal word processors at home, and of these 61% reported using them for New Year cards and letters, while 41% used them for an extension of company work (Kyanon Hanbai 1988).

These figures could indicate that despite the 90% take-up rate of the new technology it had really only had superficial application, or that, as the survey was aimed specifically at men, perhaps the main users of the word processor in a professional manner were female staff. The 1981 company case studies discussed earlier in this chapter make it clear that it was mainly the female staff who used the machines, even in the one company that had set out to include male staff members as well. A 1983 survey of office automation also found that women were more likely to use office automation equipment than men, with the only exceptions being mainframe and personal computers which were more frequently the preserve of male staff. The function of women was predominantly that of entering data: in other words, they were involved in 'information transfer' as opposed to 'information production' (Morris-Suzuki 1988: 118, 120, 130). Apart from their gender implications, the other interesting point about the Canon figures is that they indicate that 20% of men at managerial level were now able to use word processors, where the 1981 case studies indicated that use was concentrated in the lower levels.

Outside the office

The new technology thus made early inroads - to varying degrees - into offices. Its adoption by personal users, however, was at first a little slower. This was due in large part to the previously mentioned business orientation of the internal dictionaries of early word processors, which necessitated extra work for users wanting words perhaps from literary or historical fields. The other factor, of course, was cost. With early machines costing millions of yen, only businesses could afford to purchase them. It was not until 1981 that several companies came down to the one million yen mark; in 1982, Fujitsu's My Oasys machine dipped below it.

The appearance of the My Oasys first started high school teacher Yokoyama Masami thinking about solving his bad handwriting problem by investing in a word processor. It was clear, he said, that the My Oasys was targeted at the individual for personal use because the name incorporated the pronoun 'my' (as in other Japanese advertising phrases like 'my car', 'my home', indicating personal ownership), the size was smaller, and, at 750,000 yen, it was cheaper than other models. When Fujitsu followed the My Oasys with the even smaller My Oasys 2 at a cost of 480,000 yen in 1983, he decided to buy one (Yokoyama 1984: 65–67). This 'handwriting complex', as we shall see in a later chapter, was instrumental in persuading many people to buy a word processor in Japan, as elsewhere.

The move to personal use came about largely because Japanese buyers were charmed by the novelty of the comparative ease and efficiency with which they could now type their own language. They also liked the ability to store material in files and recall it as required, and the ease of editing written work. The second and third of these functions were not unique to Japan and merely put the Japanese word processor on a par with those used in the west. It was the first which was the real drawcard: people now had access to a machine which would allow them to type 'proper Japanese' (ie including kanji) through a simple conversion process without any lengthy special training. The time required to write a manuscript, send it off to be typed or printed, receive it back for checking and then have the corrections retyped was now greatly shortened by being able to do it all oneself on one machine. Errors deriving from the writer's poor handwriting or mistakes not picked up by others could be eliminated in the process (Fujisaki 1984: 111). For the first time people in Japan had a machine with which they could rapidly transform the ideas in their heads into printed Japanese text.

Kabashima Tadao, then of Osaka Prefectural University, reflected on the usefulness of the word processor from the viewpoint of a university lecturer rather than an office worker. He compared it to the photocopier, which had reduced labour by allowing quick copies, reductions and enlargements of texts. Unlike the photocopier, the word processor could not be used straight away without a week or so of training. Once the user had mastered it, however, it had far more labour-saving advantages than the copier. There was no longer any need to look up in a dictionary those kanji that one could not quite remember how to write; the word processor would provide suggestions from which to choose. It could also be caused to store particular kanji in memory to avoid the task of selection next time round. Writing a manuscript for a journal article or book required both intellectual and manual work: the word processor would of course take care of most of the manual side of things, but could also be induced to undertake some of the intellectual tasks as well, as was evinced by the fact that one could write a document without consulting a dictionary. Another example was the use of macros to call up frequently used words or phrases at the touch of a key, where the intellectual exercise of translation was left to the machine (Kabashima 1982: 84–86).

Umesao, who as we saw in Chapter One was a keen proponent of document automation, was one of those unimpressed with the business orientation of the internal dictionaries when he began to use a word processor in the spring of 1982; it seemed to him inappropriate for academic purposes. If one input the word 'shohyō', for example, hoping to get the characters for 'book review', the word processor's first offering would be those meaning 'various lists' instead, as one would expect in an office context. Because of his view that characters were a hindrance, Umesao, despite his belief in the need for automated document production, was not unreservedly in favour of the way in which the word processor worked overall. While he praised its editing potential, he called for the removal of the kana-kanji conversion function, believing that the expense of providing this function was responsible for the fact that the Japanese word processor did not have as many editing functions as its western counterpart (eg it could not make an index). The fall in price, which some hailed as a defining moment for Japan's language culture because it brought the new technology within the reach of the average earner, Umesao attributed to a cutting of editing functions which reduced what should have been one of the biggest advantages of the word processor. He suggested that the kanji conversion function should be replaced with other editing functions. The word processor would then use hiragana, with spaces between words, with some katakana and romaji and perhaps a very few kanji. In other words, what he wanted was a Japanese typewriter with high-quality editing abilities on a par with the western word processor, and he saw characters as the barrier to achieving this. Without the kanji conversion function, the cost involved in supplying it could be diverted to improving other functions (Umesao 1988: 239–240).

The lack of historical place and personal names in the dictionaries limited the usefulness of the early machines for academic and literary work. 'Ieyasu', the personal name of Tokugawa Ieyasu (first shogun of the Tokugawa dynasty), for example, was not included in the dictionary; the two characters had to be input separately, and tracking down the second, less common character took quite a lot of time and effort. One way to find it was to think of a compound word in which the character occurred, call it up, and then delete the unwanted part. Unfortunately, not many compounds contained the 'yasu' kanji in this particular instance. Since it was not in the word processor's dictionary under the reading 'yasu', attempts to find it under its other reading of 'kō' resulted in a list of more than ninety characters, all pronounced 'kō', which had to be searched for the right one (Tezuka 1984: 66–67).

This matter of the dictionary was therefore one that greatly exercised the minds of users as the popularity of the machine grew. In this context, of course, the term 'dictionary' refers not to a dictionary in the sense of a lexicon which supplies meaning for words, but to the internal dictionary of the word processor which matches up kana input with appropriate kanji equivalents for the conversion process. The word 'appropriate' is a key term here: in many cases the dictionary ran into some trouble in early word processors with knowing where to cut the kana input into words, resulting in many mistaken conversions with, at times, totally meaningless output, ie character combinations which represented no known words. The one thing most necessary for accurate conversion was a good dictionary, one that had a high probability of providing the desired characters on a first attempt.

A further complaint about early dictionaries was that they contained only short words, owing to considerations of space and time: if all the short words and the longer words of which they also formed part were included in the dictionary, the efficiency of conversion would be reduced by the need to search through so many words for correspondences with kana. People who did not know about the 'short words only' aspect would try unsuccessfully to input three-character words like 'jitensha' (bicycle) and 'jidōsha' (car) for quite some time before resorting to breaking them up into component parts. While very long words need not be included, some felt, common words such as the two cited ought to be included in the dictionary even at the price of a little overlap (Satake 1983: 32). Today, of course, they are.

After 1987, when Sharp first introduced artificial intelligence (AI) into its dictionaries, the situation improved considerably. Early word processors had operated on a single-word conversion method, ie the operator would key in a word and immediately press the conversion key to obtain a kanji equivalent. Soon after, a more sophisticated conversion of several words at a time was achieved, and later a successive autoconversion system which automatically converted chunks of input. None of these, however, was free of conversion mistakes, and the AI dictionary was developed to try to overcome this defect. With earlier versions of the dictionary, the kana input of 'atsui' (hot/thick/serious) might not produce the appropriate choice of character from among the homophones. In an AI dictionary, the correct kanji for 'atsui' (hot) would be linked in one set with related nouns such as tea, hot water, soup, iron and so on; that for 'atsui' (thick) would be placed in sets with words such as wall, floor, book and so on; that for 'atsui' (serious) would be paired with words describing illness. Thus the likelihood of mistaken conversions was greatly diminished (Tanaka 1991: 53–55).

There was and is no standardisation of dictionaries among different makes of word processor. The contents of each manufacturer's dictionary are a trade secret, not revealed in order to keep a particular edge on the market. Not that new dictionaries are compiled by manufacturers, of course; to create a dictionary from scratch for the word processor would take many years, and new model machines come out much more frequently than that. Manufacturers refer to a number of existing dictionaries and to other data such as lexical surveys carried out by the National Language Research Institute in Tokyo. It is unclear what exactly is meant when a manufacturer's advertising material claims that the dictionary of a particular model contains a certain number of 'basic words': some manufacturers count conjugated forms of verbs, for instance, as separate words while others do not. It is therefore still a good idea, as it was ten years ago, for intending purchasers to investigate the matter of the dictionary with some thoroughness before making a decision.

A continuing trajectory

We saw in Chapter One that sales took off in 1984, continuing to rise during the 1980s until by 1991 approximately around one in four people owned a word processor, and that figures for that financial year indicated that 32.6% of all households owned a word processor, an increase from 24.1% in the 1989 financial year. What were the demographics of this diffusion? Analysed by household type, the findings were that 28.5% of farm households had a word processor, up from 19.2% in 1989; 33.8% of workers' households, up from 25.7%; and 34.9% of proprietors' households, up from 24.5% (Japan Statistical Association 1992: 548). By 1993, 37.8% of all households owned a word processor; the proportion of workers' households had risen to 40.9% and of proprietors' households to 39.9%, but in farm households the proportion had dropped to 26.4% (with a 200% jump in the number of farm households with personal computers, to 9.3% from 3.8%) (Japan Statistical Association 1995: 588). The technology was being used across a wide spectrum of society. By the early to mid-1990s, word processing in Japan was firmly established both as a pivot of office automation and as a tool for personal use.

The 1980s saw the rapid spread of the technology, then, but it was still in that first decade largely viewed as a matter of convenience and/or personal choice. In the 1990s, however, businesses set up whole information processing networks predicated on electronic characters, which meant that employees, particularly in the newspaper industry, had no choice but to use word processors and personal computers as terminals. This was the era of *denshi moji*, electronic characters processed by computers, replacing the on-paper printed or handwritten characters that were still predominant in the 1980s. The word processor, because its 'product' was a document printed on paper, was considered by many to be no more than a stand-in for the pen and was used as a tool within that conceptual framework. Yet even as a tool within a handwriting world, its extreme convenience meant that it spread rapidly, thereby acting as a catalyst for the shift to electronic characters in the 1990s (Tanaka 1991: 22–23).

This technology, by bringing about the transition from direct-to-paper characters to on-screen characters which pass through several modes and loci of handling before arriving at the printing stage, achieved a kind of liberation of text from all but the final exigencies of paper. It has been suggested, rightly in my view, that the Japanese word processor is a representative icon of Japan's success in technology, the invention which established Japan's independence as a technological innovator providing solutions to overcome local problems: 'The Japanese word processor is a product of independent Japanese technology, not an imitation of something European. It evolved and developed through competition between businesses, and has influenced kanji countries such as Korea and China and other countries which do not use the roman alphabet to produce word processors for their own languages. If there is one striking product which demonstrates the coming to independence of Japanese technology in the 1980s, that is probably the word processor.' (Tanaka 1991: 57)

It is clear that electronic handling of characters, either on word processor or personal computer, is here to stay as a part of everyday life in Japan. The following chapter will examine in detail the changes in written Japanese, by which I mean predominantly the use of script, which are perceived as stemming from this. It will also examine the relevance of this phenomenon to the existing script policy of Japan and any changes which might be indicated for the future.

CHAPTER THREE

Changes in Writing Habits and their Implications for Script Policy

With such a radical breakthrough in the handling of Japanese script occurring over a relatively short period and spreading so rapidly, it was only to be expected that people would voice concerns about changes in the nature of written Japanese which followed on from the use of the new technology. The specific focus of those concerns was how script, and in particular kanji, was now used. The switch from what had been a culture of handwriting to one of easily produced print gave rise to fears that the nature of text would be transformed in unacceptable ways; this had to be balanced against the clear advantages of the word processor for handling and storing text. The debate over the first fifteen years ranged from the mere listing of the quantifiable changes already observable (or already perceived as occurring, despite lack of hard evidence) to broader concerns about changes to the overall language system of Japanese. This chapter will examine these concerns and the implications of any substantive changes for Japan's existing script policy.

Increase in number of printed documents

One of the most immediately noticeable changes has of course been a great increase in the number of printed documents in circulation. Within the office, as we have seen, all manner of business documents which were formerly handwritten before being typed up can now be produced comparatively easily in printed form from the first draft. Outside the business world, many manuscripts of all kinds, from novels to conference papers to university and school essays, are now printed rather than handwritten. So are postcards bearing New Year and other seasonal greetings, and to a growing extent even personal letters. This is largely due not only to convenience of production but also to ease of reading: no longer must the recipient or reader, eg a printer, struggle with deciphering poor handwriting and near-illegible editorial corrections. As early as 1987, half the manuscripts received by the well-known literary journal Waseda Bungaku were written on word processors (Kida, Furuse et al. 1987: 169). Some of the increase in printed documents stemmed from a desire to alleviate the practical consequences of poor handwriting: a 1994 NHK television program, 'Kurabete mireba: tegaki vs wapuro' (Comparisons: handwriting vs word processor), for instance, reported that 49 out of 50 test postcards addressed to NHK using a word processor were correctly processed by the automatic mail sorting machine at the Shibuya Mail Exchange in Tokyo, whereas only 29 of 50 handwritten versions made it through.

There have also been changes in the appearance of text. One of these, as we shall see, relates to an increase in the number of characters used. Other changes worth noting here are an increase in horizontal writing (*yokogaki*) from left to right, as opposed to the traditional vertical writing (*tategaki*) from right to left, and an increased density of text. The former trend has become particularly noticeable in the writing of younger people since the mid-1980s, when various surveys revealed them to prefer horizontal writing. While most early word processors could produce vertical output, they often could not show it on the screen; this led many users to choose the horizontal format instead (Ogino 1987: 32). This is not a particularly radical change, given that horizontal writing has been commonly employed since the war in a variety of government and scientific contexts. The text of newspapers, magazines and books, however, is written vertically, as are many people's letters. In 1991, a survey of 114 students at Tsukuba University conducted in order to determine how university students used the word processor returned 35 reporting that they often wrote horizontally and 56 that they mostly did so. The main reason given was that this was how the word processor screen displayed text; many indicated that they would still write horizontally even if not using a word processor. While word processor use may therefore have promoted *yokogaki* to some extent, there seems to have been a clear trend in that direction in any case (Ogino 1992: 34–35).

The age of the user may also be a contributing factor in decreasing a feeling of resistance towards small characters. Word processor print is usually much smaller than handwriting, and much more information can be fitted on to a page, perhaps giving older people used to the larger print of moveable type the impression that the page is over-crowded. What used to need a sheet of notepaper now requires only a postcard. This ability to fit in more information because of the size of the print led one hopeful writer to postulate a saving in postage fees as a spin-off benefit of word processor use (Horii 1990: 61).

As to whether the elusive concept of the style of a document changed when its creator used a word processor, some reported a belief that in fact their writing became more "logical" than if they had written by hand. One such was non-fiction author Yamane Isse, who believed that when he wrote by hand his writing had a vitality that came through clearly when it was read. Text written on a word processor, however, tended to be more logical, because it was written in the knowledge that sections could be inserted or deleted at will (Mori, Yamane et al. 1988: 19). This flexibility, of course, is probably one of the most profound influences on style, since it allows thorough editing and polishing much more easily than handwriting. A document no longer has to be fully conceptualised from the start: the writer can start from any section and build in the others later. This can be the proverbial two-edged sword, though, because if the sections are not well blended the result can seem disjointed and fragmented. Some creative writers have suggested that the word processor is best suited to writing scientific or academic articles and books, which depend on logical development of an argument; others, such as Abe Kōbo and Sono Ayako, relate that they have successfully used it to write works of fiction with no ill effects on style.

Standardisation

What if word processor users, faced with the sometimes circumscribed choices offered by the machine's in-built dictionary, are too pressed for time, or too lazy, to take the time to key in the extra strokes needed to arrive at the version they prefer? Would this lead to a kind of defacto 'standardisation' of writing which would lead in turn to uniformity in orthography and loss of individuality? Personal style, this argument ran, could become a casualty of convenience because of the limitations of the dictionaries, which often did not contain the latest colloquialisms or offer the preferred orthography in the conversion choices. Kuratani Naomi, professor of information linguistics at Matsukage Joshi Gakuin University, for example, was critical of the failure of early business-oriented word processors to supply katakana versions of words in the dictionary. His own personal preference was to write the word 'boku' (I) in katakana, but to get the word processor to do this necessitated several extra key strokes: he had to actually type the word 'boku' in katakana from the keyboard rather than being able to type it in romaji or hiragana and have the katakana version come up on screen as one of the conversion options. 'It's absurd', he complained, 'that companies should subjugate our language, our most precious heritage, to their own commercial policies in this way' (Hagiwara, Nakamura et al. 1988: 14). There is of course nothing to stop users from bypassing what the dictionary suggests and keying in their own choice manually, as Kuratani could have done by typing the katakana 'boku' straight from the keyboard and pressing the 'no conversion' key. Arguments of this kind appear to centre on convenience, where convenience is defined as the minimum time and effort needed to achieve the desired result. Even a few simple keystrokes assume an importance out of proportion to the time taken when compared to the 'glamour' of the instant conversion process.

As we saw in Chapter Two, the 1980s saw considerable criticism of the limited nature of the dictionary by non-business users. The most frequent requests from users, apart from the inclusion of more characters that we shall examine later, were for more colloquialisms and greater choice of orthographic variants for particular words. The kana-kanji conversion process focused on written language (*kakikotoba*) using modern kana spellings (ie, the modern kana usage instituted as official usage in the postwar script reforms). This did not allow people to mix colloquialisms with prewar kana spelling at the same level if they so desired, or in general to play with the language as they pleased. A wealth of literature on the subject indicates that users wished for greater choice than was then available, despite the possibility that including all the options across a range of styles in the dictionary might make the conversion process less efficient.

One of the central issues here is the matter of *okurigana*, the question of how much of an inflected word should be represented by a character (or characters) and how much by hiragana. Despite the existence of an official government policy designed to standardise usage ('Revised Rules for Using *Okurigana*', 1973), *okurigana* use in practice varies from person to person, depending on individual preference. This has been attributed to the lingering influence of childhood habits – whichever form was given in a person's childhood primary school textbooks, which depended on which of the two (1958 and 1973) official policies was in at the time (older people, of course, grew up in the days when there was no official policy at all). Some people, as a result, like to use fewer *okurigana*, others prefer more. Two often-quoted examples are the words 'okonau' (to conduct, carry out) and 'toriatsukai' (treatment, handling). Some people write the former as '**oko**-nau', others '**okona**-u', while the latter could be either '**to**-ri-**atsuka**-i' or '**toriatsuka**-i' (where the bold print represents the section or sections of the word written in kanji and the plain print the appended hiragana, known in this context as *okurigana*). Both the VJE and the Matsutake front-end processors supply both versions of the examples given above. The developers of Matsutake had at first intended to include only those forms found on the official list. On reflection, however, they had decided that they should include both, as many people did not choose to conform to the list for reasons of personal preference. In the case of 'okonau', even someone who normally appended only a hiragana 'u' might occasionally decide to add a 'na' as well in the case of the past tense '**oko**-natta' to make it clear that what was meant was not the word '**i**-tta'(went) (same character, different pronunciation, different meaning) (Hagiwara, Nakamura et al. 1988: 13).

What did people mean when they said 'fear of standardisation'? The term 'standardisation' in this context was not referring to the official policy on *okurigana*, which of course sets out suggestions for a standardised version. It referred rather to the fact that the word processor dictionaries, particularly in the early stages, offered only one alternative, eg only '**no**-ri-**mono**' (transport) and not '**norimono**' as well. What was necessary, warned Ibaraki University professor Ishiwata Toshio, was to take care to avoid being too compliant in accepting whatever choice the word processor offered first whether or not it accorded with the user's own wishes, resulting in a kind of defacto standardisation, a 'word processor-suggested orthography' rather like the 'chef's suggestions' found on some restaurant menus (Ishiwata 1988: 18). In cases such as this, one can always enter one's preferred variant by typing in the component parts separately, but there is a strong tendency to accept what the conversion key offers rather than take the extra trouble. This, it was felt, might lead to a uniformity of writing which in itself would not be a bad thing if the word processor were always correct, but many times it was not; manufacturers should enter various options into the dictionary and leave the choice to the user (Ogino 1987: 33).

This, in fact, was already happening by 1987, when a survey of seventeen different word processors was conducted in order to discover what results the conversion process of each gave for the same sets of words. A check on *okurigana* results showed a wide variety of offerings for the same word, often involving not only different *okurigana* but different kanji as well. When the verb 'tobidasu'(run out, jump out) was input, for example, nine machines gave only '**to**-bi-**da**-su'; one gave the choice of either '**to**-bi-**da**-su' or '**tobida**-su'; two gave '**to**-bi-**da**-su' but with two different kanji choices for the '**to**' segment; one combined all three; one gave '**to**-bi-**da**-su' and two versions of '**to**-bidasu', one with each of the two different '**to**' kanji; one gave the four choices of '**to**-bi-**da**-su'and '**tobida**-su' with the first of the '**to**' kanji and the same two variants with the second; one gave '**to**-bi-**da**-su', '**tobida**-su' and '**to**-bidasu' with the first kanji and '**to**-bidasu' with the second; and one gave '**tobida**-su' with the first of the '**to**' kanji and 'tobi-**da**-su'. The official script policy specifies '**to**-bi-**da**-su', but also permits '**tobida**-su'. Clearly, the word processor dictionaries were observing the rules, but no indication was given by the order in which choices were offered of which were the official forms and which the recognised variants to help those who were unsure (Endō, Kuwabara et al. 1987: 107).

The issue of consistency, of course, has all sorts of ramifications for Japanese in the computer age. Even where government script policies specify certain variants, in practice usage is diverse and wide-ranging, and this diversity has traditionally been cherished. It became clear, however, that it posed problems where computers were concerned. Some felt that the answer lay in establishing a *seishohō*, a fixed way of writing Japanese which allowed for no variation and would facilitate computer manipulation of the language. Multiple variants make machine translation or database searching much harder. If one wished to search a database for articles pertaining to *okurigana*, for instance, inputting '**oku**-ri-**gana**' would bring up only those articles in which the word written in precisely that same way featured in the titles. Titles containing other versions of 'okurigana', eg '**okurigana**' (three kanji only), '**oku**-ri-**gana**' (with a different character for the 'ga'), '**oku**-rigana', or the word 'okurigana' written entirely in either hiragana or katakana without kanji would be missed (Nomura 1991: 34). Book titles (say) containing the prewar equivalent of a character later simplified in the postwar script reforms would not show up if the search term input used the modern simplified version. So long as there was no one standardised form in use, the search terms would have to be widened to include all possibilities. In a sense, the advent of the word processor provided a good opportunity to think carefully about how words were written. So convenient was the conversion function, however, and so rapid the development of the market, that issues such as these were not given the full consideration they deserved.

The fears described above are predicated upon a view of the user as unwilling to take the time and trouble to key in his or her personally-preferred variation when the word processor conversion function offers something different. In early word processors, perhaps, when the novelty of the conversion process dazzled many, when dictionaries did not offer as many choices as they do now, and when the 'learning' function which remembers which form is most likely to be used was not as developed, there may have been some grounds for fearing such an outcome. It is of course the user who is in control of the machine and not the other way round; not the machine but the person at the keyboard decides what the eventual output will be. As we shall see, various later studies have shown that the more experienced users become the more likely they are to take the trouble to instruct the machine in the kind of orthography which best suits their individual tastes, and to save those preferences.

For every writer in the literature who called for standardisation, there were two or more who resisted the idea, emphasising this issue of user responsibility as of paramount importance in any approach to the possible effects of using a word processor. For example: standardising the orthography would place a limit on the expressive powers of the language. Whether a person's manner of writing changed after they began to use a word processor rested on the habits of the person in question, not any properties inherent in the machine; therefore, as long as the users themselves were intellectually and culturally active, they would not be influenced by any limitations the word processor might have (Fujisaki 1984: 115). Or: there had never been another period in the history of written Japanese when such determined autonomy in establishing individual style was required as now. The word processor was above all just a tool, a writing implement, which it was now the duty of those engaged in intellectual production to master. The use of the tool was not in itself an end. Care must be taken that the written Japanese of the future did not end up as insipid, lacking all individuality, through foolish standardisation (Atsuji 1991: 224). In other words, the user must take responsibility for the final product of his or her engagement with the word processor rather than allowing the process of using the machine to bulk so large that it obscures this duty. Diversity was still seen as more important than conformity to a uniform standard, no matter how desirable that might be from the machine point of view.

Kanji overload

The most immediately apparent changes in documents relate to various aspects of kanji usage. It was also in this area that perceptions of changes being wrought in the language initially ran riot. To enable a clearer sense of the issues, it is useful here to delineate four main areas on which comment has focused: the overuse of characters; the revival of very complex characters; the proliferation of mistaken character choices for homophones; and the fear that word processor users would forget how to write kanji by hand.

The first of these, the perceived **overuse of kanji** because of the ease with which they could be called up by the conversion key, occasioned comment right from the beginning. As users have become more experienced, however, this has become less of an issue. In the 1980s, the novelty of at last being able to print out kanji without first going through the complicated process earlier described with the Japanese typewriter led many users to convert words into characters which would normally, in handwriting, have been left in kana. Part of this was due to early conversion systems which required activating the conversion process for each word rather than, as now, allowing the conversion of longer units. Kanda Yasunori, introduced in Chapter Two as one of the developers of the first Fujitsu word processors, owned to feeling responsible that the simplicity of the conversion function had resulted in an overuse of characters (Kanda 1984: 88). The JIS character levels contained many more characters than were needed for ordinary manuscripts. With this level of choice, some asked, how was one to decide the extent to which kanji conversion should proceed?

Whether due to immature conversion technology or lack of user control, the increase in the proportion of characters in word-processed documents led to the complaint that such documents were unacceptably 'black', an impression produced by the fact that most characters contain many more strokes than kana and thus look denser on the page. An article assessing the impact of information technology on the language gave an example of this by rewriting a paragraph of text overusing the conversion key. Words such as 'kono yō ni' (thus), 'dō' (how), 'naru' (become), 'iu' (say), 'mono' (thing), 'kore' (this), 'aru' (be) and so on, normally written in kana, were converted into kanji instead. The writer rightly believed this would be a short-lived phenomenon; as word processing technology developed beyond short conversions only to conversion of longer text segments the problem would disappear (Ishiwata 1988: 17–18).

Another who agreed with this view was Tsukuba University's Ogino Tsunao, who has researched and published widely on the effect of word processing. Beginners, Ogino argued, tended to use a lot of kanji at first because their sloppy technique meant it took them longer to seek out and hit the correct keys. Not wishing to waste the time and effort they had expended, they were apt to accept whatever kanji came up rather than use their own discrimination to select only those which were appropriate. As they became more accustomed to using the word processor, however, their technique improved and they then developed a more discriminatory attitude to selection (Kida, Furuse et al. 1987: 148).

Some saw the trend to more characters as a return to the past (to the prewar situation, when there were no official attempts to control character use). Word processor manufacturers made the fact that the dictionaries contained large numbers of characters a selling point for their products; both manufacturers and users were happy with this situation. The result, however, was that people were over-using the conversion function and characters were appearing in places where it was not necessary to use them. Given the choice between using kana and using characters, most people would opt for the latter because they had been taught in school that using kana was a temporary intermediate step on the way to learning characters, the correct and adult way to write. In schools, children learning to write Japanese were encouraged to use as many characters as possible. Until now, the difficulty of remembering and correctly writing too many had limited their use, and had led to the development of official script policies; the word processor, however, had reversed this. What it all boiled down to was the need for self control on the part of the user (Umesao 1988: 234,238).

A 1991 cultural history of intellectual production which examined the kind of world which might result from the introduction of word processors also commented on this propensity of manufacturers to include large numbers of kanji in the dictionary as a sign of a high class machine. A small survey which the author carried out on user attitudes revealed a definite perception among respondents that word processor use had led to increased kanji use. This had led to a revival of non-modern usages, such as for example, writing 'arigatō' (thank you) in kanji instead of kana. Putting native Japanese words such as 'ashita' (tomorrow), 'kinō' (yesterday) and 'ototoi' (the day before yesterday) into kanji blurred the nuanced distinction between words of native origin and words of Chinese origin (Atsuji 1991: 207). Often the issue of character use was simply a matter of vocabulary choice: if Sino-Japanese words (normally written in kanji) were used in preference to native Japanese words, the natural result would be an increase in the proportion of characters in the text.

One who opposed the increase in characters vehemently from the start was Ishida Tamio who, as a member of the Kanamojikai, saw no need for characters at all. Early on, Ishida wrote about an example from a piece of text used as an advertisement for a Toshiba word processor, which was packed densely with characters. For purposes of comparison, Ishida rewrote the passage as he himself would have written it, using far fewer characters and spaces between words (Ishida 1979: 100). A comparison of the two pieces reveals the trade-off between using different proportions of characters. Ishida's rewrite is somewhat longer than the original, underlining the fact that one reason characters are valued is for their conciseness, for the ability to convey a lot of information in a couple of characters which would need many more symbols were the words written out in kana. The other aspect is his perceived need to use spaces between words (one of the key proposals of the Kanamojikai): another argument often advanced in support of kanji is that they offer visual clues to morpheme boundaries and thus enable

Japanese to be written without word spacing. Kanji pack in more information than words written in hiragana, katakana or romaji: a large number of kanji and Sino-Japanese words are found on the front pages of newspapers not only because such words occur more frequently in the fields of politics and economics, but also because of the conciseness of expression they make possible. This of course is directly related to the amount of space available on the newspaper page (Nagata 1989: 67).

Journalist Tanaka Ryōta attributed the increased proportion of kanji to laziness or ingrained habit on the part of users rather than over-enthusiasm. As a cadet journalist in 1965, he recalled, he had been instructed to restrict the proportion of kanji in his writing to around 30%. Because journalists use a large number of proper nouns (written in kanji) in their articles, they need to take care not to use too many other characters in the rest of the article in order not to give text the 'black' look referred to earlier. There was also a common consensus that too many characters made text harder, not easier, to read. As a result, he had become accustomed to writing many words of Japanese origin in hiragana. When he began to use a word processor, he was surprised to find that it offered kanji equivalents for such native Japanese words as 'sore' (that), 'chōdo' (exactly) and 'kore' (this), among others, and even a kanji for 'lettuce', usually written in katakana. Tanaka calculated that if he had accepted all the kanji the word processor threw up as first choice, the proportion of characters in his articles would have risen to between 60 and 70%. In office deskwork, he noted, the thing which most exercised people dealing with manuscripts written on word processors was the overload of characters. Many writers who had been using word processors since the early days when they could convert only one short segment at a time had never got out of the habit of pressing the conversion key after each unit even after they had upgraded to more advanced machines which could handle longer segments. Tanaka thought it a pity that designers of the machines still gave priority to characters, causing users to have to go through all sorts of operations to put words back into hiragana. In late 1989, he recalled, he had asked manufacturers whether, given the advance to complex conversion, they should not now leave words generally written in hiragana in hiragana (without offering kanji versions). The manufacturers had replied that while they saw his point, the whole point of the word processor was precisely that it was in fact a machine which could change hiragana to kanji. It was not just technicians who thus gave priority to kanji, Tanaka reflected, it was the consumers as well (Tanaka 1991: 133–135). Such a comment suggests that the technical designers of the word processor saw its application not in terms of producing Japanese text appropriate to contemporary norms but rather in terms of a mechanical push-button substitution operation aimed more at script conversion than anything else, in isolation from overarching concerns of appropriateness.

Very little survey research has been done to confirm or deny perceptions of an increase in kanji, and certainly none on a scale which could provide a basis for definitive generalised judgements on whether or not a change in Japanese orthography is under way on a national scale. In many of the multitude of articles and books read in the course of this research, statements along the lines of 'there are no objective statistics/ there is no real research, but . . .' occurred with monotonous regularity. What surveys have been done are limited in their range, but may nevertheless provide us with small packets of valuable information. One such was carried out by Ogino, who in 1992 conducted a survey of 687 experienced word processor users. Of those who answered the question on whether or not they used a greater proportion of characters when writing with a word processor, 125 respondents confirmed that they did, with only twelve replying that they used fewer (Ogino 1994: 10–11). This contrasts, however, with the findings of another researcher's small survey carried out the previous year, which revealed that despite the widespread belief that word processor use led to an increase in kanji use, respondents actually reported a small decrease in the proportion. This survey did not deal with perceptions based on interviews or questionnaires of users but was rather a computer analysis of published articles written pre- and post-word processor use by writers who themselves were writing about word processors. For each writer, the text of a post-word processor article was compared with that of one written before the author had begun to use a word processor. The results of the analysis showed that whereas the average rate of kanji use pre-word processor was 30.94%, the post-word processor rate was 30.62%, representing a very slight drop. In only a couple of articles had there been a rise (Tsuruoka 1991: 7–8).

There is some evidence that rates of kanji usage in the community at large are dropping anyway, and it is possible that electronic character retrieval may counteract this. Ogino cites a survey by Yasumoto Yoshinori in which one hundred novels written between 1900 and 1955 were analysed. Over that half-century, the rate of kanji use in the texts was found to have dropped from 39% to 27%. If this rate of attrition were to continue at the same pace, Yasumoto predicted, kanji would disappear entirely by the year 2191. Ogino quoted other surveys to show that the rate of kanji use among young people was declining, including one which indicated that the proportion of kanji in the *manga* (cartoons) so widely read in Japan was as little as 18.7%. Only time would tell whether or not word processing would reverse this trend, but indications were that users were already counteracting the trend to overuse by exercising greater autonomy (Ogino 1987: 32).

Revival of complex kanji

A second aspect of kanji use which claimed attention was the **revival of very complex kanji**, or of older kanji which had dropped out of use. There were good reasons why these characters were no longer used; the postwar script reforms had aimed at limiting the characters in general use, so that many considered excessively complex in structure or representing words of Japanese origin which might better be written in kana (some pronouns and postpositions, for example) or only used in obscure words were no longer taught in schools. One such character is the twenty-six-stroke second character in the word 'yūutsu' (melancholy). A second example is the word 'kirei' (beautiful), written since the war in kana but now often seen in characters (eight strokes and nineteen strokes). For older people educated before the 1946 script reforms, the reappearance of these older characters may not pose such a problem. Younger people, however, will not be able to read them; one writer commented that when he wrote the word 'tsumabiraka' (clear, detailed) in kanji, his thirty-something research assistant did not know how to pronounce it. This word is of native Japanese origin and if written in kana is instantly recognisable (Yamada 1989: 1105).

What has happened here is that the word processor dictionary has 'reacquainted' people with characters they might otherwise have forgotten or never knew in the first place. Most people can read more kanji than they can write; just knowing the word does not mean being able to recall the correct kanji. If this situation arises when one is writing by hand, a decision has to be made as to whether to look up the dictionary, leave the word in kana or substitute a different expression. No such decision is necessary if one is using a word processor, however, as the conversion process can easily locate the characters in the dictionary and produce them correctly whether or not the writer remembers their correct form and stroke order.

The only way to avoid the appearance of these characters is to take steps to see that they are not converted from kana, usually by pushing the 'no conversion' key, or, in cases where one half of a word is written with a well-known character and the other with a very complex one, by observing the practice enshrined in the first postwar character list of *mazegaki*, or writing one half with the character and the other half in kana. The 1946 List of Characters for Interim Use, prescriptive in nature, had decreed that where a particular character did not appear on the official list it should not be used. When a word was of Japanese origin this caused no particular problem, but for Sino-Japanese words, which were normally written with two or more characters, it led in some cases to awkward half-and-half representations of words. The previously-cited 'yūutsu' (melancholy), for instance, was written in this way, with the difficult 'utsu' character replaced with kana, as was 'sentaku' (laundry), where the first character was on the list and the second was not. To many people, these *mazegaki* words were a blot on the orthographic landscape caused by over-zealous restriction of character use, and the ability of the word processor to provide characters for both halves of the compound without the stress associated with remembering how to write them by hand was a welcome development. The proliferation of *mazegaki* after the 1946 list came into force and was adopted by government organs and, voluntarily, by newspapers had been one of the reasons advanced in support of weakening the prescriptive nature of the list and increasing the number of characters it contained, resulting eventually in its replacement in 1981 by the List of Characters for General Use. With the word processor so convenient, it was unlikely that *mazegaki* would appeal as an alternative to using the full characters.

One side benefit of this encyclopaedic nature of the word processor dictionary is that the Atsuji survey referred to earlier in this chapter showed that many of those who used word processors found themselves through exposure becoming familiar with the readings of kanji that they did not know before. These respondents reported that often, through repeating the conversion process over and over on the screen, they eventually learned the relationship between the kanji displayed on the screen and the reading. Typing in the name 'Kaoru', for example, brought up more than just one character option, including some older characters – through seeing these other characters each time that particular conversion was performed, even though they did not select them, they became for the first time aware of how to pronounce them. Atsuji himself believed that if the word processor continued to spread among young people, its screen would provide that generation with another method of familiarising themselves with kanji outside the classroom, and that could only be a good thing. Knowing even one more kanji than was taught in school would be an advantage in accessing the cultural heritage of the past, because so many young people could not now read the characters in the works of (pre-script reform) great writers such as Natsume Sōseki and Mori Ōgai (Atsuji 1991: 202–204). This increased reading ability is, as we shall see, important in terms of its implications for the debate about possible future changes to script policy consequent upon the spread of word processing.

Kanji mistakes: *ateji* and *muimigo*

An undesired by-product of the conversion process has been the proliferation in writing, particularly among young people, of ***ateji***, where somebody chooses a character or characters from the list provided by the word processor with the same pronunciation as the word input in kana or romaji but with a different meaning. This can sometimes happen with *kun*[1] readings, but it mostly occurs in compounds where the characters have the same *on* reading, hence the word *dōon igigo* (same *on*, different meaning) for 'homophone'. Where the characters meaning 'negotiation' are wanted, for example, careless or over-hasty selection might result in the printing of the characters for 'refined', both words being pronounced 'kōshō' and input as such from the keyboard. This, of course, comes about because of the large number of homophones in Japanese, which in turn is a result of the relatively small number of Sino-Japanese morpheme shapes. Statistically, about one third of the words in the dictionary have homophones (Nomura 1986: 69). Further statistical data is provided by research carried out by the National Language Research Institute in Tokyo. Its table lists the top eight words, ie the eight words with the most homophones. First comes 'kōshō', with 28; then 'kikō' and 'kōshi' (27 each), 'kōki' (24), 'senkō' (23), 'kōka' and 'shisei' (22 each), and finally 'kōkō' (21). Forty-five kanji have a *kun* reading of 'ka', 44 of 'o', 42 of 'to', 38 of 'I', 'su' and 'ha', and 35 of 'ko' (cited in Yokoyama 1984: 65). Yoshida Susumu, researching word processor dictionaries, charted the relationship of the degree of overlap between words and homophones in a general-use dictionary he and his colleagues created: of a total of 29,321 words, 21,010 had no homophones, but the remaining 8,311 had between two and fourteen each (with two words having as many as eighteen) (Yoshida 1984: 29). Given this large number of homophones, it is not surprising that all word processor users have stories to relate about problems in this area. The literature is replete with anecdotes detailing frustration and, in some cases, misunderstanding.

In 1982, it was predicted that until word processing technology developed to the point where it could discriminate between homophones, as opposed to the existing system where one character was suggested first and the user selected alternatives from a supplementary list if it were not the one wanted, there would be a flood of *ateji* because people did not want to take the extra trouble to select the correct characters. If in a certain context expression A were appropriate but even expression B would convey the general meaning, users would probably choose B if more keystrokes were required to select A than B. People brought up on the *maru-batsu* (right-wrong) system favoured by the education system would not hesitate to snatch a similar-looking character if there were one, even if they harboured doubts about its appropriateness (Mizutani 1982: 24).

The homophone problem, attributable to the paucity of syllables available in Japanese (111 counting the nasalised 'g' syllables in the Tokyo dialect, compared to, say, 2,500 in Korean), takes various forms. First there are those which are far apart in meaning and unlikely to appear in the same context, such as 'kaihō' (liberation) and 'kaihō' (open). As words of this type are on the whole different parts of speech and/or are used in different contexts, they are unlikely to cause confusion. Then there are those which are close in meaning and apt to be confused with each other, such as 'kitei' and 'kitei', both of which mean 'regulations' but have one character different. Some words likely to appear in the same context and cause confusion if mixed up are 'shiritsu' (municipal) and 'shiritsu' (private), and 'kagaku' (chemistry) and 'kagaku' (science). Finally, there are words which are basically the same word but are written with different characters; there is only a minuscule difference in meaning, and they are either used as the same word, eg the two versions of 'gogen' (etymology), or in different contexts, eg 'onwa' (mild) written with one set of characters to describe the weather and with another to describe a person's temperament. These examples are all based on characters which have the same *on* reading but different meanings; there are also words which have the same *kun* reading (ie words of native Japanese origin) and different characters. Again, some of these have different meanings and are used in different contexts and are therefore easy to distinguish, eg, 'arawasu' (to indicate) and 'arawasu' (to write), and some are closer in meaning and liable to be confused, eg the two versions of 'koeru' (pass), one of which means 'to go past something' and the other 'to pass a certain limit' in an abstract sense (Nagata 1989: 71–72).

It is not hard to see why people might be either unwilling to hunt through lists of homophones to find the right one when another fairly close in meaning might do, or (particularly for younger users) simply not know the meanings of all the options. And, of course, having to slow down to make the appropriate choice reduces the overall speed with which a document can be produced; given that one of the advertised benefits of the word processor is that it saves time in document production, people in a hurry may resent having to spend time arriving at the correct choice of characters. The 'learning' function helps, of course, and the advances in artificial intelligence since 1987, in which words are paired in the dictionary with other words most likely to be linked with them in certain semantic or grammatical contexts, have also done something to halt Mizutani's predicted flood of *ateji*. In the final analysis, of course, mistakes of this kind are the fault of the user. A word processor is after all, it cannot be emphasised too strongly, just a machine. No matter how many thousands of characters its memory stores, if the person using the machine does not know which of the alternatives to choose, mistakes will occur. Users need to work from the basis of a sound knowledge of kanji to get the best from this technology.

A second cause of textual mistakes, much more noticeable than *ateji*, was the propensity of the early word processors in particular to cut up the kana input wrongly, resulting in dictionary conversions which were totally meaningless (***muimigo***, meaningless or nonsense words). Cutting up strings of kana into the correct syntactic units is the biggest problem in achieving correct conversion. Just as sentences written in kana only are not easy for people to read, so they pose a problem for the word processor as well. *Bunsetsu*, as we saw in Chapter Two, are the smallest possible syntactic units into which a sentence can be divided. They are composed of *jiritsugo* (free forms, ie parts of speech such as nouns, verbs, adjectives, adverbs and so on) and *fuzokugo* (bound forms, ie particles and auxiliary verbs). If these *bunsetsu* units are correctly recognised and converted by the word processor, then the rest is just a matter of differentiating correctly between homophones, and the 'learning' function can help with this. If the segmenting is wrongly done, however, the user has to correct this by moving the cursor to the appropriate place and starting again. An experiment was conducted to measure the abilities of the kana-kanji conversion system as a mechanism for handling natural language, using the widely-used VJE-β front processor first marketed in 1986. While this processor was found to be in general fairly effective, there were nevertheless problems of mistaken conversions resulting from incorrect gauging of the length of the *bunsetsu*, confusion of the dividing line between a noun followed by a particle and the next unit (resulting in, for example, 'onaji/ toki wa' being converted as 'onajito/ kiwa'), and other mistaken readings (Ogino 1989). An amusing example of mistaken conversions may be found in the advertisement for Sanyo's Wapuro Hakase V. What should have been converted to 'yudetamago ga daisuki' (I love boiled eggs) was mistakenly converted to 'yudeta mago ga daisuki' (I love boiled grandchildren). Not all have this element of humour, however; the same advertisement lists several other examples of misresolution, which it claims the new 'intelligent' Hakase (Expert) word processor will prevent (no author given, 1996: 26).

A further investigation of the *muimigo* problem was provided by an experiment which tried out thirteen different models of word processor, all manufactured between April 1985 and March 1987, in order to ascertain the rate at which their conversion processes produced nonsense when contemporary words from the 1982 Sanseido dictionary were typed in. The Casioword HW-900F, for example, with an internal dictionary size of 110,000, produced 88 correct conversions and 42 meaningless ones; the Canoword 350 (71,000) 100 correct and 116 meaningless; the Toshiba Rupo 70FII (45,000) 82 correct and 186 incorrect, and so on. The nonsense words thrown up in the survey fell into three classes. Some were simple sound correspondences without regard to meaning. For example, when the word 'karakami' (bamboo paper) was input in hiragana, three characters with the readings 'kara', 'ka' and 'mi' might appear but bearing no relationship at all to the meaning of the word 'bamboo paper' – the three might mean instead 'empty', 'add' and 'beauty' respectively. A second type might combine characters which appeared perhaps to be proper nouns because they ended in the characters for 'Mr.' or 'city ward', but in reality no such personal or place name existed. Finally, there was the noun 'karasu' (crow), which had been treated as if it were a causative form of a verb, resulting in unlikely forms such as the characters for 'ka' (hunt) or 'ka' (cut) followed by the hiragana 'rasu'.

The best conversion rate discovered in the machines tested was 82.7% (ie 82.7% correct conversion) for the Canoword 360. The lowest was 53.4% for the NEC NWP-5V. In some cases there were found to be differences between different models put out by the same company depending on price and time of manufacture. Comparing the Canoword 350 and 360, for example, where the 360 was marketed about four months after the 350 and cost about 20,000 yen more, the correct conversion rate went up from 75.2% to 82.7% in the 360 and the dictionary appeared to have been improved (from 71,000 to 110,000 words). Toshiba's machines showed a similar difference in the performance of the more expensive model: the Rupo JWR100, marketed in March 1987 for 198,000 yen, performed significantly better at 77.4% than its stablemate the Rupo 70FII, marketed only a month earlier for 70,000 yen less (61.7%). Again, the dictionary capacity was different: 45,000 words for the cheaper machine and 63,000 for the more expensive. On the other hand, both the Sharp Shoin WD600 (September 1985, 330,000 yen) and WD630 (October 1986, 285,000 yen) achieved exactly the same rate of correct conversions (80.5%), although there were some slight differences in which words each would convert.

The experiment found 42 words (of a total of 133) which converted without any problems. Thirty-eight of these were Sino-Japanese words, and four were native Japanese words. Of the 133 words tested, 88 were Sino-Japanese, 43 were Japanese words, and two were a mixture. On the whole, then, it was harder to achieve a correct conversion of a Japanese word than a Sino-Japanese (Endō, Kuwabara et al. 1987: 68–80).

In connected text, the problem of *muimigo* arises when the word processor dictionary does not correctly interpret the kana input in terms of the *bunsetsu* described above. To look at a simple example from the experiment; the sentence 'ame ga furisō da ga, watashi wa dekakeru' (it looks as though it's going to rain, but I'm going out) is composed of the *jiritsugo* 'ame' (rain), 'furi' (fall), 'watashi' (I) and 'dekakeru' (go out), and the *fuzokugo* 'ga'(subject marker), 'sō da' (it seems), 'ga' (but) and 'wa' (topic marker). The sentence could therefore be divided into four *bunsetsu*: 'ame ga' (rain), 'furisō da ga' (looks likely to fall but), 'watashi wa' (I) and 'dekakeru' (go out). (Note that there are spaces between these words when romanised but not when written in Japanese.) When typing this sentence on a word processor, the desired conversion result for the first of these would be the kanji for 'rain' with a hiragana 'ga' for the subject marker; for the second, the kanji for 'fall' (of rain) with the hiragana for 'risō da ga'; and so on. When this sentence was typed on the Canoword 350, however, two different kanji with the reading 'ame' were supplied, only one of which meant 'rain', and the 'furisō da ga' conversion produced eight options, one of which was correct, one of which gave a different kanji for the verb, and six of which were utterly meaningless correspondences of characters to syllables on the basis of pronunciation (eg the characters for 'not' (fu), 'advantage' (ri), 'sect' (sō) and 'field' (da), with a hiragana 'ga'). The software manufacturers appeared to lack a proper understanding of the concept of *bunsetsu*, with the result that conversion was a very hit-and-miss, uncoordinated affair (Endō, Kuwabara et al. 1987: 95).

Interestingly, the experiment further showed that the correct-conversion rate of *shakai yōgo* (social terms, ie words relating to government, economics, welfare) surpassed that of *kaji yōgo* (household terms, eg food and clothing), with success rates of about 80% and 50–60% respectively. No matter which machine was used, an area-related bias was found in the conversion capacity, with household terms coming in second. Since many of the social terms are shorter than the household terms, the higher conversion rate might have come about because shorter words are easier to convert correctly than longer ones. Regardless of the machine, conversion success declined as the word got longer, but differences in the ways in which individual machines searched might have accounted for this. The decline in the successful conversion rate as the number of characters in the word increased was more pronounced in the household field than in the social field. Two-kanji words relating to food and clothing were harder to convert properly than four-kanji social terms in some cases.

This bias in the fields as reflected in comparative conversion rates, the researcher concluded, was perhaps due to a judgement on the part of the manufacturers that household words were more specialised, less likely to be used than social terms. But the word processor was no longer just used in offices. At the time of the experiment it was found in three million homes and was used by housewives and people in a wide range of fields for a wide range of purposes; this judgement, therefore, was surely no longer valid. A rational dictionary program, free of bias towards certain fields and reliable in giving correct and rapid conversions for words in general daily use was needed now. Software design should not rely on technology alone but should also incorporate the views of specialists in language use who would apply objective and logical selection criteria (113–114).

In light of the difficulties with *ateji* and *muimigo*, it clearly cannot be said that a change from handwriting to word processing produces a less stressful process of document production for either writer or reader. A high number of incorrect conversions is irritating for a word processor user, who then has to redo the segment with extra keystrokes until the desired result is achieved. In a sense, this is the psychological equivalent of the often-cited physical disadvantages of handwriting: sore shoulders, cramped fingers and ink stains. These physical disadvantages are traded off against the mental indigestion caused by *muimigo*. For the reader, the annoyance of finding wrong conversions, usually not *muimigo* but *ateji* produced by careless or hurried writers, equates to the stress of deciding whether or not to look up a forgotten character in a dictionary when handwriting. While every medium carries with it its own inbuilt problems, in the case of the word processor, mistaken conversion is one that bulks large in the public eye.

Forgetting kanji

Underpinning all these other concerns about erosion of correct kanji use has been the deeper fear that word processor users may **forget how to write kanji** altogether if they stop writing by hand, much like the decline in mental arithmetic skills attributed to the use of calculators. A somewhat extreme version of this fear, particularly in the early days, was that the word processor would become so integral a part of daily life, even outside the business world, that people would lose the ability to write characters altogether. Atsuji's survey, mentioned earlier, reported that many people found they were now unable to write kanji which had given them no trouble before; some denounced this as the word processor's greatest 'crime' (Atsuji 1991: 202). And in Ogino's 1992 survey of 687 experienced users, referred to above, of those who answered the question relating to loss of kanji skills 328 replied that they had indeed begun to forget characters since they had begun to use a word processor, while only 27 replied that their kanji skills had in fact been reinforced (Ogino 1994: 10–11). This section will examine some of the views expressed on this topic.

Some people, for example Ishiwata Toshio of Ibaraki University, worried somewhat fancifully about the possible unwanted side-effects of producing school materials on a word processor. It was fine for class handouts and examination papers to be printed rather than handwritten, he felt, if that prevented teachers from making mistakes, but the practice might lead to teachers forgetting the characters when they tried to write on the board (something attested to by many lecturers who were keen word processor users, eg Ogino 1990: 21, Kabashima 1989: 7). When a word processor is used for teaching materials, if the page is enlarged on a copier the notches and bumps on the dot matrix characters become clearly visible. If children were told to write using these copies as their model, would they perhaps reproduce these notches, thinking them to be how the character should be written? If so, the end result would be that they would lose an understanding of the beauty of characters (Ishiwata 1988: 18).

The Kanamojikai, of course, dedicated to the abolition of characters, viewed the prospect of forgotten kanji skills as a cause for rejoicing. Japanese was under the control of characters to such an extent, one member wrote, that the true form of the language was rapidly being lost (Yamasaki 1984: 13). Another, Tatsuoka Hiroshi, believed that the practice of writing characters by hand was bound to decline as the word processor spread; if people did not write by hand, they would grow gradually more uncertain of the accuracy of their recall of the strokes of characters. Tatsuoka viewed the popularity of the word processor as a temporary phenomenon. True, there were those who argued that it would ensure the survival of kanji, but the Japanese were gradually losing their ability to use characters properly. It might seem interesting at first to be able to call up complex characters, but in the long run people would not use those they were not sure of (Tatsuoka 1984: 9). Yet a third Kanamojikai member, Yamashita Taketoshi, denied that the stand his group had taken against kanji had ever been based solely on the grounds that they were inefficient and that in consequence their main argument had now been demolished. Their basic belief, he affirmed, was that expressed above by Yamasaki, that the Japanese language had been distorted by the Chinese influence (epitomised by characters) over a very long period of time. The primary aim in fighting for the abolition of kanji was therefore to protect the Japanese language as just that, the Japanese language, not a Sinified variant. To abolish characters immediately would be impossible, however, and therefore the advent of a convenient machine such as the word processor which would go even a little way toward solving the problems caused by kanji was a fine thing (Yamashita 1983: 4).

Some universities which had introduced word processors in the early 1980s reported declining kanji reproduction skills in their student population. An article which appeared in the Asahi Shinbun on 23 September 1985, for example, reported that since the full-scale introduction of word processors on a campus in Isehara, more and more students were finding it increasingly difficult to write even quite simple characters by hand. The kanji skills students had possessed at high school exit level seemed to be eroding because of word processors. Of course, noted the writer, there had been evidence for some time of a decline in the number of characters being used by young people in general; if the word processor continued to spread, this might exacerbate the trend a great deal. The situation on this particular campus had now reached the point where the university, which had formerly insisted on printed assignments in an effort to inculcate potentially useful word processing skills, had changed its policy to require students to submit their graduation theses first in handwriting and then later in printed form, in order to redress the problem of disappearing kanji skills.

Reflecting on this article, Katō Jizō, a professor at Showa Women's University, questioned whether word processor use alone sufficed to explain the deterioration in kanji proficiency once a student reached university. Like Ogino, he attributed the fact that the students made the specific kanji errors mentioned in the article to the fact that their kanji skills were low in the first place, rather than to the medium used. To support this thesis, he analysed a pile of two hundred reports handwritten by his students, in which he found many *ateji* mistakes and mistakes in radicals. If a student were unable to write properly in the first place, Katō argued, then that student would have no greater success on a word processor, since output naturally reflects proficiency (Katō 1985: 33). This argument might hold true for *ateji*, where it is a matter of pressing a key to choose between alternatives and where inferior knowledge of which characters are correct might result in mistaken choices, but it is more difficult to sustain with regard to the second of Katō's findings, the mistakes in radicals. A word processor *cannot* give an incorrect radical: once the key is pressed, the correct form of the character is chosen, so that in this sense the machine might be seen as actually helping those with insufficient knowledge to write the correct radical to turn out acceptable characters.

In the survey of Tsukuba University students referred to at the beginning of this chapter, the students by and large had not begun to use word processors until they arrived at university. Eighty-six had their own word processors (81 being stand-alone models rather than PCs with software). Since their individual orthographic styles were not at that point fully formed, the way they wrote was apt to be unconsciously affected by the word processor's first choices, often because they were not yet sufficiently familiar with the machine to know about functions which would enable them to impose their own wishes. Most of them used their word processors for things related to their university work, such as research essays or lists of references, and wrote other things such as letters, address lists and memos by hand. Thirty-two students indicated that they had begun to forget kanji, as opposed to four who felt that using a word processor had helped them to remember characters better. The longer a student had been using the word processor, the more likely he or she was to indicate a drop in kanji skills (Ogino 1992: 37, 39).

The kind of research Ogino, who conducted the Tsukuba survey, would like to see done is a longitudinal study which takes into account the influence of age, the fact that an individual's kanji skills change over time regardless of whether or not they use a word processor, and the fact that some people write in general more fluently than others. An ideal survey might be of university students whose kanji reproduction skills could be tested upon entry and then later upon graduation, with details being taken of their experience with a word processor in the years in between. A comparison of these two results would probably give a fairly accurate picture of the influence of the word processor, at least on a group of young people (Ogino 1990: 20–21).

It must be noted that not everyone sees loss of kanji writing skills as an altogether bad thing (and I am not here referring to the advocates of kana or romanisation). One major argument is that the use of the word processor, while people *may* forget how to write kanji properly, frees up time spent on character drills for learning other language skills such as expressive writing. It does not matter if some characters are forgotten, because the machine supplies the correct version. Ogino, for example, wants all his students to use word processors because in his view their advantages outweigh the possible disadvantage of forgetting a few characters. Even at primary school, he believes, where it might seem that word processor use would be counter-productive because students of that age are meant to be actively learning kanji, the benefits which it offers in, say, composition classes are enough to more than make up for lagging kanji education. It is better to use a word processor than to write laboriously by hand, and better for children to extend themselves in different areas of writing than to try to remember the correct stroke order for characters and whether a stroke hooks up at the end or not. Given that many adults routinely replace complex characters with hiragana when they write, teaching these kanji seems meaningless; assessment then really just boils down to exams for exams' sake. Kanji dictation questions are popular in entrance examinations because they can easily be marked right or wrong, but they are not really a good test of language ability; that surely depends not on how many characters a person knows but on their skill in using them in context. Word processing may lead eventually to a lessening in importance of such assessment techniques (Kida, Furuse et al. 1987: 153–155). Children will inevitably forget some of what they have learned about writing kanji by hand; the introduction of calculators had a similar effect on the study of arithmetic. While it is important to understand the structure of calculations, nobody ever now considers doing actual complex calculations by hand. In the instrumentalist view, word processing is in essence the same. Teachers should therefore view word processors not as the enemy of kanji education, but as a positive means of increasing children's creativity (Ogino 1987: 34–35).

As usual, there are two ways of looking at this issue. One is to say that using the machine makes the actual process of writing itself more interesting, thus drawing out people's abilities. The other is that since it is the writer who does the thinking and not the machine, which is no more than a conduit, word processor use will not help composition ability at all. The latter of these arguments, which harks back to the 'user responsibility' refrain we have seen in earlier sections of this chapter, seems to have greater validity. It may be that what proponents of the former are really thinking of is improved presentation. What university lecturer, for example, has not become familiar in recent years with the beautifully presented, impeccably formatted assignment adorned with computer-generated graphics which looks wonderful but says very little, while a less flamboyantly presented essay may present an information-packed, logically argued case? Not that there is always a strict correspondence between the two, of course, but in some cases, format and adornment are used to disguise a lack of content. Has the use of a computer with word-processing software here really 'drawn out the abilities of the student' in a way than enriches their writing, or merely contributed to making the document look more exciting?

Of course, we must not forget that the actual process of learning to write through extended practice plays an important role in fixing characters in memory so that they can later be recognised. Any advocacy that word processors should be used in primary schools, apart from in such composition-based activities as production of class newspapers, either overlooks or dismisses this too lightly. The NHK television program referred to earlier ran a test, dividing forty primary-school children into two groups and having half learn some new characters by using a word processor and half by handwriting the characters. A dictation test was then administered: fifteen of the twenty in the handwriting group attained a perfect score, while not one of the twenty in the word processor group did. The program then moved on to test the role of hand movement in adult recognition of characters. First, test subjects were asked to guess which character was being described by a description of its component parts. In each case, the subjects were observed moving their fingers in their laps in the practice of *karagaki* (tracing characters in the air), and were successful in guessing the required characters. For the second part of the test, however, they were asked to place their hands, unmoving, on the table and again tell the interviewer which character was being described. Without the help of the hand actions, neither was able to correctly visualise the shape. From these two experiments, it is clear that handwriting, the learned sequence of hand movements which results in production of the character, plays a significant role in recall.

To short-circuit the process of ensuring recognition through cutting back on handwriting practice would thus be counterproductive, because it is this very skill of recognition which is most important in enabling correct use of the word processor. If a user cannot distinguish between the characters thrown up on screen by the conversion process to the extent of being able to choose the correct one, then, as we have seen, he or she will produce text riddled with mistakes. Even if someone cannot remember how to reproduce a certain character correctly by hand, they can still produce a document provided that they can tell whether the correct kanji is shown on the screen; after that, it is just a matter of hitting the key to select it. The crucial element, therefore, is the ability to *recognise* the characters: with a word processor, remarks Fujitsu's Kanda, one cannot write at all unless one can first read characters (Kanda 1984: 88). It was fear that the role which handwriting plays in learning to read characters would be diminished which contributed to the reluctance of many Japanese teachers to introduce computers with word processing software into the classroom. Teachers maintained that simply seeing characters on screen without writing them as well was not enough to learn them properly, and feared that computer use would produce a generation of school children who could not write characters; this resulted in a low level of computer diffusion in Japanese schools (McGregor 1995).

By 1991, we find Atsuji writing that the whole matter of kanji skills needed to be kept in perspective. While it certainly appeared to be true that those who consistently used word processors gradually lost their ability to write kanji correctly, it was also true that the conversion process, by throwing up alternatives, made people aware of characters they either could not read or did not know before. The word processor had by 1991 spread to such an extent that the things which caused comment when it first appeared, such as printed rather than handwritten New Year greeting cards, had come to be taken for granted. The new technology was merely an improved writing implement; it had also brought about a fundamental change in the way in which Japanese was written. History offered several examples of an existing culture being radically changed by the appearance of a new writing implement, such as the development of paper; people only began writing long sentences after the advent of the fountain pen. Thanks to the new word processing technology, modern Japanese were now experiencing for the first time the major change in the intellectual production environment which it had wrought. Seen in this light, the question of how Japan's language culture would change over time was revealed as complex and could not be addressed simplistically (Atsuji 1991: 203, 227).

Overall, the kanji skills issue is neatly encapsulated by an automotive metaphor provided by Fujisaki Hiroya, who likened the word processor to a car: born of technology and undergoing constant improvement. Like a car, which enables easy and rapid movement of people and materials, the use of the word processor leads to speed in writing, which in turn expedites the circulation of information. On the other hand, just as there has been an increase in traffic accidents, so there is also the risk of an increase in poorly written documents and the spread of inaccurate information. The use of the car has meant a weakening in the strength of the legs; so also, use of the word processor could reduce the ability to write and remember difficult characters. The development of this type of machine and the dependence on them which results in a lowering of people's abilities, whether we like it or not, is an unavoidable fate for the human race, and to deny this would be to deny the entire history of civilisation (Fujisaki 1984: 115)

The changing view of kanji and implications for script policy

Along with all this debate on aspects of kanji has gone significant reflection on the overall role to be played by characters in the information age. Kana supporters found it odd that people should say that the new technology obviated the need for further script reform. The number of kanji in general use had decreased since the Meiji Period, true, but the burden of characters in the education system had not – characters still required a disproportionate amount of time to learn, which kana advocates believed could be better spent on widening the parameters of general education (eg, Takahashi 1983: 6). This point of view – that characters should be abolished – found no favour with the general community. The advent of the word processor, however, did herald a change in perceptions of the nature of kanji, with consequent calls for a revised approach to character education to bring it more into line with the perceived needs of the electronic age, moving away from the current premise that characters are handwritten.

The main thrust of this argument is that characters ought no longer to be taught for both recognition and reproduction equally, but rather that a greater number ought to be taught for recognition only and a reduced number for reproduction. How much value is there in the word processor age, asked academic Kabashima Tadao, one of the most prolific writers on this subject, in spending time memorising how to write large numbers of characters and in being able to write them by hand? Surely, given the ease with which the memory of the word processor could supply them, it makes sense that they should be done by machine and not by hand. A large character set with many complex forms is more suited to production by machine than by human beings, who suffer physical side-effects such as sore shoulders, fingers and necks as a result of writing by hand (Kabashima 1988: 25). Many others agreed with him (eg Kida, Furuse et al. 1987: 157; Kanda 1984: 88; Yokoyama 1984: 66).

Given that the word processor can now produce thousands of characters very easily, why is there any further need to have an official script policy which designates a limited number of characters for general use? The policy currently in force is the List of Characters for General Use (*Jōyō Kanji Hyō),* which suggests as a general guideline using 1,945 characters for ordinary social documents, excluding specialist fields. This policy was preceded by an earlier, more prescriptive list of 1,850 characters, the List of Characters for Interim Use (*Tōyō Kanji Hyō,* 1946), which was the outcome of a long process of attempts to arrive at a government-authorised script policy which had spanned almost half a century (see Gottlieb 1995). Central to the debate was the issue of whether a limit should be put on the number of characters in everyday use, and, if so, what it should be. The argument which eventually culminated in the postwar lists, which were part of a larger cycle of script reforms which also included modernisation of kana spelling and simplification of character shapes, was long and bitter. On one side were conservatives, who feared that the transmission of the nation's cultural heritage would be damaged by any change to the unfettered prewar orthography; on the other were progressives who saw character limits, and in some cases the total abolition of characters, as essential to the educational and economic progress of the nation. The invention of the word processor, which defeated the obstacle of memory to reproducing characters, has been welcomed by proponents of the former position because it appears to challenge the need for restrictions.

There are clearly still arguments in favour of limits, not least being that a certain fixed number of basic characters must be taught in schools if the nation is to maintain its standards of literacy. What good would it do to return to a situation where unlimited numbers of characters appeared in texts if many of them could not be read without recourse to a dictionary? Which characters ought to be taught during the period of compulsory education to ensure that all students receive a uniform education in reading? In any case, there are no prescriptive limits in force: the foreword to the List of Characters for General Use makes it very clear that the list is not a *seigen* (limit) as in the case of the 1946 list but a *meyasu* (guide), and is not intended to be at all binding on the individual. The only areas where it is binding are those which form part of the government, for example the ministries, which are bound by the fact that the list was officially proclaimed to stick to its parameters in government documents. As the Ministry of Education is one of these, of course, this means that all textbooks must also conform to the List.

Yamada Hisao, who as we have seen advocates romanisation, finds the argument for increasing the number of kanji because of the word processor a strange one. Should the number of characters increase, for instance, the number of homophones - bugbear of the word processor, as we have seen - would also increase (Yamada 1989: 1004). The idea that the word processor is above all an instrument for writing well, ie in clear and concise Japanese, has not yet taken root in Japan, Yamada believes. In 1989, he criticised the National Language Council for not undertaking any high level investigation of this but concentrating instead on whether this or that character should be included in the list. What was needed was a long-range plan and a searching discussion of how Japanese should be written rather than a focus on micro issues such as character usage (Yamada 1989: 1106–1107). As we shall shortly see, the Council is now investigating issues relating to the use of the language in the information age. At the time of Yamada's comments, however, it had not yet finished the 25-year cycle of review of the postwar reforms begun in 1966 and was still engaged in consideration of matters relating to kana spelling and how foreign loanwords (excluding Chinese) should be written.

In fact, as we know, the number of characters held in word processor dictionaries is not determined on the basis of the national script policy, although occasionally people have suggested that this should be the case. If it were, dictionaries would hold little more than the 1,945 on the List of Characters for General Use, supplemented by characters used in personal and place names which do not appear on that list. This would not even allow sufficient scope to produce newspaper and magazine articles. What word processors contain, as we saw in Chapter Two, are the first and second levels of the JIS (Japan Industrial Standards) characters, a total of 6,355, decided not by the Education Ministry as in the case of the script policy list but by the Ministry of International Trade and Industry (MITI).

The method of selection of the JIS characters has been criticised as reflecting an odd, conservative view of language based on mechanical measuring of frequency rather than any understanding of the needs of intellectual life. The selectors chose characters from such lists as the *Kokuritsu Kokkai Toshokan Shūyō Kanji Hyō* (National Diet Library Received Character List) and the *Jōhō Shori Gakkai Kanji Kōdo Iinkai Hyōjun Kōdoyō Kanji Hyō Shian* (the Information Processing Society Kanji Code Committee's Draft Plan for a Kanji List to be used for Standard Codes). These large lists, however, did not deal with frequency; although the 'sō' of the name of famous and frequently cited author Natsume Sōseki did not appear in them, a very esoteric and seldom used character from a phrase relating to the Imperial House had been fitted in. It all boils down to how people think about Japanese culture. What is needed, some suggest, is not an 'industrial standard' set of characters but a 'literature standard'. The JIS lists should not be focused solely on office culture and authoritarianism while remaining deaf to literature and the arts. They were compiled with no real understanding of what a word processor would be used for in the wider community. Scholars of the Chinese classics or researchers in Buddhist scriptures likewise find the characters contained in Levels One and Two insufficient: the characters for some Chinese personal and place names are not available. It is not just that writing about foreign cultures cannot be fully accommodated with the JIS characters; the needs of Japan's own culture cannot adequately be met either. Many of the old characters needed for writing about Japanese history, for example, are found in neither level of JIS. Only a few people might need them, but they are necessary to the proper description of historical aspects of Japanese culture; one cannot substitute other characters without distorting the facts of history (Kida, Furuse et al. 1987: 41–44). Likewise, it is not possible to write about early classical literature such as the Kojiki or the Man'yōshū without using certain characters not on the list (Atsuji 1991: 220).

As a result of calls for the list to be extended, and in particular as a result of pressure from the printing industry, the supplementary list of a further 5,801 JIS character codes was issued in 1990. Even in the days of the prescriptive *Tōyō Kanji* list, the printing industry needed to use a large number of extra characters. As no private user or printery was constrained to stay within the boundaries of the list, which affected only government printeries, when customers requested that certain characters or character forms be used in an order the printer would comply, even to the extent of going to buy type for any not already held. Things changed, however, when writers began to bring in manuscripts on floppy disks instead of bringing handwritten or printed-out versions. Since the printery then had to handle the disk with its own company computers, any characters not on the existing JIS list caused confusion in the printing process because the two computers assigned them different codes. It was to redress this that the JIS codes were extended to assign standard codes for a further 5,801 characters, to enable computers to talk to each other when these characters were used (Nomura 1991: 31–32).

It was only to be expected, of course, that the prime mover in the selection of the JIS characters would be the office world rather than the more specialised needs of different intellectual fields. As we saw in Chapter Two, the JIS codes were devised in order to standardise the exchange of information in Japanese text between computers and word processors. Their primary consideration therefore related to the technical rather than the linguistic aspects of the matter, and the JIS committees were composed mainly of people from industry rather than linguists. A few years ago, when compatibility between different makes of word processors and word processing software for the personal computer became a reality by using the MS-DOS conversion function, it was the JIS standards which enabled this to happen by providing a standardised set of character codes; if each individual word processor and personal computer manufacturer had been using their own codes for characters rather than a standard set, it would not have been possible. Given that the concern was to get computers to talk to each other in a comprehensible fashion by assigning an unchanging code to each character, and that those in charge of the deliberative process came from the backgrounds they did, it is understandable that the first thrust concentrated for the most part on characters which were of more immediate application than, say, historical nomenclature which in many cases involved characters no longer in common use.

So the fact that the word processor dictionary contains so many characters does not in itself mean that all kanji problems are now solved. Handwriting allows a person to use any character they choose, no matter how obscure; with the word processor, if it is not in the machine, it cannot be used. In this sense, although the word processor at first glance represents newfound freedom in the matter of characters, in reality it is not as flexible as the earlier culture of handwriting.

Whether or not a word processor user who is not a specialist in some field or other of study would ever actually need all the characters available in the word processor (ie, in JIS Levels One and Two), of course, is open to question. A survey done by the National Language Research Institute on changes in the vocabulary used in the magazine Chūō Kōron over a seventy-year period found that 97.5% of the total number of characters which appeared in the 1976 data were found on the List of Characters for General Use. If a person who were only able to read the characters on that List were to read that year's issues, for every 1,000 characters which were used they would know 975. Those figures relate to the total number of characters used overall. In terms of the total number of *different* characters used, there were 1,664, of which 85.6% were on the list. If a word processor contained only the 1,945 characters of the *Jōyō Kanji*, as some had advocated, it could be used to type only 85.6% of the characters used in the magazine. The *Jōyō Kanji* List, therefore, does not contain quite enough characters for writing at the level found in a modern adult-oriented magazine, which various other surveys have found to be about three thousand (Tanaka 1991: 59–60).

Tanaka Akio looked at rank ordering those three thousand by frequency of use in order to determine how useful a word processor which contained all of them would be for typing text for today's newspapers and magazines. He compared the data from three surveys: characters from modern newspapers (1966, National Language Research Institute), characters from modern magazines (1956, National Language Research Institute), and characters from the early Showa Period[2] (1932–38, Ōnishi Masao). In the first survey, the first three thousand characters accounted for 99.9% of the total, the first two thousand for 99.4%, and the first five hundred for 79.4% of the total used. In the second, the first three thousand characters again accounted for 99.9% of the total. If a word processor contained those three thousand characters, the possibility of coming across a character it could not produce would therefore be only one in one thousand. Even if it only contained the first two thousand, there would still be only four characters per thousand which could not be typed. Since some characters only used in personal, place or company names were included in these figures, and some which figured only in such things as titles of plays or books, somebody typing ordinary text which did not have any special bent could get by with the 2,965 of the JIS Level One (Tanaka 1991: 61). These findings indicate that the 6,355 characters of JIS Levels One and Two are far superfluous to the requirements of the ordinary user, but are necessary to the scholarly pursuits of academics and intellectuals who write their books and articles on word processor. In this sense, then, when manufacturers boast in promotional material of the number of kanji their machines contain, what they are doing is marking their own product as a 'high class' machine, one which is able to deal with the demands of intellectual production as well as the common round of office work.

The other area where the JIS characters were found lacking was the area of personal names. Some people do use characters in their names which are not found on the official lists; these are usually old (ie predating the 1948 list of simplified forms for the characters on the *Tōyō Kanji* list) or variant forms. The JIS list defines these variant forms as 'two different forms of the same character'. The most frequently occurring type of variant character is one in which the number of strokes has been abbreviated; others make partial modifications to the character, or change the position of its component parts. The 'tsuru' of Tsuruoka Teruo's name, for example, is one which it is very difficult to call up on the word processor, and is sometimes replaced with the less complex variant of the character. Kabashima Tadao also reports that although he uses the ordinary 'shima' (island) character in his surname, the real character recorded in his family register has a 'mountain' radical preceding the 'island' element. This character does not have a listing of its own in Nelson's Japanese-English Character Dictionary but is given as a variant of the 'shima' character. Some of his friends use the old forms of characters for names like Hiroshi, Minoru or Watanabe. The reason people bother with these old or variant characters is because that is what is recorded in their family registers; Kabashima himself has had the experience of not having his signature accepted because he signed with the ordinary 'shima' rather than with the variant in the register. Some people also feel that to change from variant forms to what are now the standard forms of characters in their names would be to divest themselves of some distinguishing feature, of individuality, and that to simplify the characters of their surnames would be to handle the family name without due respect. This reluctance to tamper with names means that even though it is legally permissible to write register names in simplified characters, some will still adhere to old characters and variant forms. Kabashima recommends that word processor manufacturers take the emotional element into account and include variant characters if that is what ordinary people wish to use (Kabashima 1991: 25–26). He attributes the appearance of the supplementary JIS list, which contains many kanji which are variants of characters already found in Levels One and Two, in part to a realisation by manufacturers that they could not afford to ignore the wishes of the many people who wished to use variant characters in personal names and in part to a desire to export their machines to other CJK countries (China, Japan, Korea). All three CJK countries use characters differently; in order to ensure exports, the existing JIS levels are simply not enough. In other words, he sees the commercial profit motive as being behind the extension of the list rather than any linguistic motive, which is only to be expected from something put out by a Ministry concerned with industry and trade. To date, however, as we have seen, these supplementary characters have not been included in word processor dictionaries.

The 1991 word processor accreditation test confirmed rather poor results for the question in which candidates were asked to type up a list of names and discussed possible solutions. There were several reasons for the poor showing: some names might contain old or variant characters not easily recognised, the pronunciations of some might be unclear (and if the pronunciation was not known, the name could not be input in kana or romaji before being converted to kanji), and there was no guarantee that the characters for a particular name would be found in the word processor's dictionary. A person whose name contained an unusual character would be offended if it were arbitrarily replaced with a simpler form; that person had every right to expect that the full-form character would be stored in the dictionary. The problem arose not only with personal names but also place names, names of groups or organisations and other proper nouns. If the new supplementary JIS list of characters were to be added to word processors and computers, the problem of name characters would be solved and people would then be compelled to use the correct character when typing addresses and so forth. The disadvantage of having so many characters available, however, apart from the increased size of the dictionary and the presumably slower conversion time this would entail, is that users could well develop a case of the jitters over correct kanji usage – is this the right one or not? Furthermore, if someone were trying to enter a name and address into a database and were not sure of the reading, that person would have to look through all 12,000 or so JIS characters to find the character. Without some sort of search tool, adding the new characters to word processors might cause more trouble than it was worth (Satake 1991: 50–51).

But should the printing industry be held to blame for any problems which might result from the increase in characters made available through the supplementary JIS codes when what is really needed is a coherent national approach to handling characters? No, says researcher Nomura Masaaki. Information exchange and information processing are two different things: the JIS standards were basically meant not for information processing but for information exchange, as reflected in their full name (*Jōhō Kōkan-yō Kanji Fugō Kei*, a system of character codes for the exchange of information). They were meant to prevent the possibility that what company A's machine input as 'ume' (plum) would be converted by company B's code to, say, 'sakura' (cherry). All the various forms of each character would be represented by the same code; even if company A's 'ume' (modern form) came out as 'ume' (old form) at company B, that would still have correctly transmitted the pertinent information. In some cases, however, eg 'sakura', separate codes were assigned to the old and new forms, which confused the general user and led to mistakes in processing information. To avoid this, it would have been preferable to keep the JIS codes purely for information exchange between machines, avoiding the inclusion of variant forms, and develop another standard for information processing. However, the JIS standard was conceived of from the start as showing the range of characters available for information processing, and has become more relevant to the general populace than the *Jōyō Kanji* list. The committee which drew up the JIS list were not unaware of this, as they divided the characters into Level One and Level Two, Level One containing all those from the 1,850 *Tōyō Kanji* List (which was in force at the time), the additional 166 characters approved for use in personal names only (*Jinmeiyō Kanji*) and about 900 characters used in place names. The extra 95 characters which were added to the *Tōyō Kanji* list when it was revised as the *Jōyō Kanji* list in 1981 were all included in Level One, which shows that it was passively recognised that all the characters needed in general social life should be available in this level. Word processors which included only level one were sold in the early stages.

If this situation had continued, kanji use might have remained centred around the *Jōyō Kanji* list. However, when the list of characters for use in personal names only was expanded by the Justice Ministry from 120 to 166 in 1981, it was found that thirteen of the new characters were in JIS Level Two, so that word processor manufacturers then vied to sell machines which contained both levels. The non-prescriptive nature of the new *Jōyō Kanji* list, which was presented as a 'guide' rather than as a 'limit', and its exemption from scrutiny of those characters needed for specialist fields underlined the trend to more rather than less character use. With the incorporation of JIS Level Two into word processors, the Japanese people were being offered a *moji seikatsu* (orthographic life) which was premised upon thousands of characters, with the 1990 supplementary characters only reinforcing the trend (Nomura 1991: 32–33). Nomura is right that the range of available characters is a major departure from the idea of rationalising and streamlining character use enshrined in the postwar script policies. Of course, as most non-specialist documents can be satisfactorily input using around three thousand characters, there is no reason to assume that the mere availability of a large set will equate to use. The characters are there for those such as specialists in esoteric fields who need them; those without such needs will not use them. Nevertheless, the very fact that they *are* available to the ordinary person signals a shift in mindset away from the idea of restraint.

Despite his reservations on this score, however, Nomura argues that it is short-sighted to say that developments in electronic technology have now obviated the need for character limits of any kind. It is true that the potential character base stored in the word processor to a certain extent robs the idea of the *Jōyō Kanji* List of its meaning, but what makes character limits important, of course, is the issue of how many students can be expected to learn by the time they leave high school. At present, students learn the 1,006 considered most important in the six years of primary school and the remaining 939 by the end of the period of compulsory education three years later. It would be ridiculous to promote a writing system which people who have come through the normal education system could not master, as was the case prewar. And how could foreign learners of Japanese be expected to come to grips with reading and writing standards which the Japanese themselves could not attain? What he suggests is that a *seishohō*, or standard way of writing words in common use, be decided; *that* was where the significance of kanji limits would lie. This would be important not only for education, but for society at large, in this era of varied character use made possible by advanced information technology.

There is a need for consistency in the administration of character-related policies at the national level in order to redress these problems. At present, the Education Ministry is responsible for the *Jōyō Kanji* list and other script policies, the Justice Ministry for the list of permitted name characters, and the Ministry of International Trade and Industry for the JIS standards for computers. It would be preferable for these Ministries to cooperate in developing some sort of coordinated policy with input from the general populace, taking a long-term view of the future of Japanese, Nomura argues, rather than leaving script policy to a small group of intellectuals. By this latter phrase one assumes he means the National Language Council. What any such group specifically ought to consider, in his view, is the following: JIS Level One must be made the standard for information *processing* (as opposed to exchange) characters; the contents of word processor dictionaries should be limited to the *Jōyō Kanji* List; the number of characters for use in names should not be increased, and it should be policy not to use any but commonly used characters in family registers and any business requiring registrations; and permitted orthographic variants (as, for example, in the *okurigana* rules) should be abolished, so that only one standard form remains. Such changes might not be popular, but to satisfy demands for freedom of expression in small matters now would lead to much greater loss of freedom as Japan heads into the twenty-first century information era (Nomura 1991: 34–35).

Nomura's less than enthusiastic view of the National Language Council's approach to script policy is shared, as we have seen, by Yamada Hisao, who believes that in the thirty-five years from 1946 to 1981 the Council was prevented from achieving real script reform because it was controlled by people who believed in the superiority of kanji, thus fettering the future development of Japanese to the dead spirits of the past. Postwar economic progress, Yamada argues, was made easier because the script reforms simplified the writing system. When the early word processors were designed, dictionaries used to decipher difficult texts written in characters were trawled to provide the contents of the electronic dictionary and the real language needs of the information era were ignored, thanks not only to manufacturers who failed to think the issue through but to conservative consumers loath to abandon obscure characters which had taken them so long to learn. The old school, Yamada believes, has a vested interest in preserving language which continues to cast China in the role of cultural hegemon and is inappropriate to the Japan of today. Characters were used in the Meiji Period partly to avoid feelings of inferiority towards the west and partly to maintain superiority over the masses. These emotional elements remain strong in the desire to produce characters on word processors, with the result that Chinese-derived words are used in preference to simple, unambiguous Japanese words. The National Language Council (at the time he wrote) was not dealing with the needs of the new information era, which require that language be easily understood, unambiguous and easy to read and write. The Council's main concern was with the aesthetics of the Japanese language and the professed need to retain characters learned rather than to let them go (Yamada 1984: 10–14).

A further suggestion for changes to script policy came from Furukawa Sueki, who, prompted by the appearance of the JIS supplementary list, proposed a completely new list, called the *Jōhō Kanji* (the Information Kanji, as opposed to the *Jōyō Kanji*, the characters for general use). Whereas the JIS list merely collected characters of high frequency, the *Jōhō Kanji* would be scientifically researched and selected on the basis of how they transmitted information; this would greatly increase the efficiency of information processing with kanji. Within the framework of the 6,355 JIS kanji, the *Jōhō Kanji* would regulate the overlap of old and new characters and standardise them to the new form, except in those very few cases where the old and the new forms meant different things. Variant forms of new characters would be jettisoned, thereby opening up space to add more than six hundred other characters to the new list. This kind of streamlining would not only reduce numbers of characters but would allow efficient searching of databases through standardisation (Furukawa 1991: 91–92).

Some sections of the community, therefore, give either qualified or strong support for a reconsideration of script policy in one form or another. Looking at the overall picture, it is abundantly clear that some of the pillars which supported postwar script policy, such as newspaper requirements, office automation difficulties and the predication upon a culture of handwriting, have been removed by the advent of the word processor and the JIS standard. Any examination of the history of Japan's script policy shows that representatives of the press were closely involved in developing the character lists, their main motivation being to reduce the number of pieces of movable type needed to print the daily papers. The top rank newspapers, noted Hoshina Kōichi, linguist and Education Ministry official who was one of the main advocates of script reform, had a total of around 10,000,000 pieces of movable type of all kinds. Of these, 4,500,000 had to be replaced every day. The space needed to store the cases containing the type was considerable; the typesetters, who ran around holding manuscripts and selecting the pieces required were estimated to cover about eight miles a day. If the cases were overturned, by earthquake or riot or some other disaster, production could not proceed until order had been restored (cited in Uemae 1975: 172). As early as 1923, a group of twenty major newspapers announced their intention to implement character limits in their pages from September 1 that year; this initiative, however, was foiled because the Great Kantō Earthquake occurred on that day, destroying some premises and knocking over the all-important cases of type in others, so that no progress could be made for another two years. The newspapers were therefore keen to see the postwar limits enacted and voluntarily adopted them, despite being private agencies not bound by the government declaration, in order to make savings in time and labour. Since then, however, advances in newspaper technology leading to computerised typesetting have done away with the problem of type, by extension removing the need to stick to a reduced character set.

The postwar character lists were based on the principle that characters would be handwritten and were therefore to be taught for both reading and writing (recognition and reproduction). The shift away from this handwriting culture to a culture of electronic character production removes one of the imperatives for character limits and, by extension, necessitates a rethink of script policy. Rather than looking backwards, the National Language Council now needs to look forward to the developing needs of Japanese in the information society. And, as we shall see in a little while, this is just what it is doing.

If script policy were to be changed because of the word processor, in what direction should the change occur? The consensus appears to be that the *Jōyō Kanji* List, if it remains, should be expanded to around 3,000 characters from the present 1,945, but that the majority of these should be taught for recognition only, with only a small number being taught for reproduction. So long as the typist knows the pronunciation of the characters and can input that pronunciation in kana or romaji, the conversion process will take care of the output, provided that the typist can recognise characters sufficiently well to be able to distinguish between homophones. So long as the reader of a word-processed document can recognise the characters, reading comprehension is assured. There is no need to teach people to be able to write all the characters by hand. Kabashima, who as we have seen pushes this line strongly, speculated in 1989 about whether it was any longer important to be able to write kanji: perhaps all that was necessary was to be able to read as many as possible of the characters needed for communication (more than the *Jōyō Kanji*), to be able to distinguish between homophones, and to be able to write a few often-used basic characters (Kabashima 1989: 7). The *Jōyō Kanji* should be increased and a certain subset of them designated specifically for writing. This argument was also supported by prominent linguist Kindaichi Haruhiko, who also advocated increasing the *Jōyō Kanji* to three thousand.

Ōiwa Hajime concurred that teaching children to reproduce characters was no longer necessary: the word processor did not allow a person to write a character unless they looked it up in the dictionary. If this were considered acceptable, there was no need to waste a lot of time in primary school on teaching how to write characters. All that was needed was to teach students how to recognise characters in a dictionary. Characters were only taught over many years of schooling because memorising them was more efficient than constantly having to look up the dictionary while writing, but the word processor solved all that (Ōiwa 1988: 49). In fact, in the late 1980s, the publishing world witnessed a boom in the sales of large dictionaries: Sanseidō's *Daijirin*, for example, which came out in November 1988, sold 300,000 copies in two months (Tanaka 1991: 131). This has been attributed in part to the need to know the correct pronunciation of a character in order to input it on word processor.

And finally, Amano Shin'ya is another who agreed that the face of education should change with the technological imperative. The word processor had freed people from the tyranny of handwriting, from having to remember which stroke flipped up at the end, which character had a small dot somewhere, things which were completely meaningless in terms of conveying information (so long as their absence did not change the meaning of the character) and were often relics of the age of brush writing, totally irrelevant to the age of ballpoint pen and pencil. On a word processor, as long as people knew the correct pronunciation to key in, there was no need to worry about these small points so needlessly considered important in handwriting, as the machine would produce the character correctly. The energy saved by not having to write characters should therefore be diverted into learning more for recognition, and people should not be compelled to write characters beyond a certain basic level. To adopt this approach would increase the number of characters people could use without increasing the burden on students. The word processor market stood (in 1991) at three million machines a year. What sort of kanji education, Amano speculated, would children born that year be receiving in the future? (Amano 1991: 67)

The role of the National Language Council

From the above, then, which is only a representative selection of comments from among many, it appears that there is a groundswell of opinion in some quarters that technological change in document production could and should lead to reconsideration of the role of characters in daily life and, by extension, of how they are taught in schools in future. What is the attitude of the body officially charged with development and maintenance of script policy, the National Language Council, to the changes which are occurring? As we have seen, the current script policy is the product of a long drawn-out battle between would-be reformers and conservatives which occupied the greater part of this century. So controversial was the issue of character limits that when the Education Minister, responding to a conservative backlash against what were perceived as over-enthusiastic restrictions on script, directed the Council in 1966 to re-evaluate the postwar script reforms, it took until 1981 to come up with the current List of Characters for General Use. Given that it took so long to arrive at a list which was a compromise between the immediate postwar reforms and those who wished to see them relaxed, it is unlikely that the Council will move with any haste to address this new issue. Nor, indeed, is it desirable that it should rush into any change in policy at this point. If the word processor (in any of its forms) becomes, as some have predicted, as widespread as the telephone (eg Tsuzugi 1984: 63), however, Japan will need to have policies in place which take account of these changed circumstances in the linguistic life of the community. To that end, therefore, the Council has in the last few years, since it reached the end of the twenty-five year cycle of reconsideration of the postwar policies, initiated measures to estimate what the impact of the new technology is likely to be.

One of the most pressing needs is for large-scale survey data to give some reliable indication of how widespread are the changes discussed above. Many of the issues are discussed in terms of anecdotal evidence, and any surveys which *have* been carried out have been limited in their scale, as their authors have been quick to point out. Ogino, whose surveys, as discussed above, have revealed some interesting results, has been calling since 1987 for surveys of a scale to allow empirically-based conclusions to be drawn. What is needed is a national survey of the scale carried out on other character-related issues by the National Language Research Institute, the body set up in 1948 to provide data as the basis of policy formulation by the National Language Council, so that some reasonably informed predictions may be formulated.

In its June 1992 Interim Report, entitled *Gendai no Kokugo o meguru Shomondai ni tsuite: Shingi Keika Hōkoku* (Various Issues relating to Modern Japanese: an Interim Report), the Council itself recognised the need for pre-emptive surveys of this kind. The text of the report ran in part as follows:

'We suggest that surveys and research are needed on the influence which the development of information technology such as the word processor is having on the way we use our language:

- information technology is extremely convenient. However, since many children have now been raised with these devices, we need also to reflect upon their downside.
- if a situation develops where text is automatically created at the touch of a button even if people do not have a good grasp of characters and words, the individual's language proficiency, power of expression and ability to think will decline. We ought therefore to undertake surveys and research before this happens and put in place the measures necessary to countermand this.' (Kokugo Shingikai 1992: 9)

The 1993 report which followed at the end of the Council's two-year term went into further detail. The development of information systems and the expansion of methods of international communication were acknowledged to be breaking totally new ground in Japan's linguistic life, with word processors, personal computers and faxes in daily use. While such technologies may be seen as adding to the convenience of everyday life, language tends to become increasingly regulated or standardised by their use. The report identified two aspects of concern: the effect of information technology upon the language, and the problem of the kanji and the dictionary within these machines.

The discussion of the first of these noted that as a result of the development of word processors and computers the social situation surrounding the use of characters is in a state of flux. It is therefore necessary to examine what sort of language abilities will be required in the future under these conditions, and in particular, what influence they will have on the ability to write itself, on the ability to write expressively, and on thinking faculties. Because the kana-kanji conversion process has made it easy to use kanji, the ability to read characters could conceivably become more important in the future.

With regard to the way in which word processors and computers use characters, the report continued, it is clear that there is some confusion surrounding character shapes. What is necessary here is to look into regulating and standardising them to conform to some sort of common yardstick, while taking into consideration the influence that this will have in various quarters. A further pressing need is to research and develop various dictionaries suited to different purposes, in line with the diversification of user objectives (Kokugo Shingikai 1993: 6). This comment about standardising character shapes would appear to be a bow in the direction of a *seishohō*, or standardised orthography; as we have seen, many consider this essential to any consideration of script in the computer age. The National Language Council, as the body responsible for rationalisation of orthography, is unlikely to be impressed by the variety of variant character forms made available by the JIS codes, and indeed did warn in the 1992 Interim Report of the problems inherent in having two standards, the *Jōyō Kanji* List and the JIS lists: 'The newspaper companies use word processors. Some characters are now appearing with different shapes from the ones we usually use. This is inconvenient. The cause appears to lie with the JIS standards. If we do not do something about this now, we face the danger that two different strands will develop in our language system' (Kokugo Shingikai 1992: 8).

The problem of character variants was taken up in more detail by the Council in its next two-year term. At its first general meeting in November 1994, the Education Minister directed members to examine how language policy in a "new era" should be constituted. One of the particular aspects to be investigated was how language policy should respond to the information era. The Council's half-term report issued a year later contained a section addressing this issue. Noting that the dissemination rate of word processing was close to double that of five years earlier, the report quoted an Agency of Cultural Affairs survey that year which had asked whether respondents had ever used a word processor or PC to produce documents or not. Only 39.9% of respondents reported that they had; 60.1% had not. Nevertheless, as more than 60% of those who answered affirmatively were men in their twenties and thirties and women in their teens and twenties, the Council considered that word processor and PC use would thereafter become increasingly the norm. It viewed the trend for a beginning user's, in particular a young person's, style to be influenced by the word processor or PC in the matter of *okurigana* and kanji use as a matter for concern. Children ought to be considered separately from adults whose style was already mature: what sort of influence did using these machines have on children whose intellectual powers and powers of expression were still developing? Rigorous surveys were needed to address these issues. The Agency of Cultural Affairs survey revealed both pluses and minuses involved in word processor use, along the lines discussed earlier in this chapter. What the Council wanted to see now was scientific research into how to use information technology so as to minimise the minuses and maximise the pluses. The report called for research and development of more versatile software (better differentiation of *yokogaki* and *tategaki*, for example) and better handling of the kanji used in basic conversions and display, all of which were seen as vital to the development of the user's linguistic skills. Large sections discussed the issues of *mazegaki*, character variants and the JIS lists, ie the sorts of issues that have been discussed throughout this chapter as surrounding word processor use (Kokugo Shingikai 1995: 439–446).

It is clear from these documents that the Council is very much aware of the ramifications of the new technology and is seeking to calculate their likely impact. It is not true, as Tanaka charged in 1991, that the Education Ministry (within which the Council is located) is avoiding the issue because it had its fingers burned in the postwar language reform debates and as a result is reluctant to meddle with the issue of character use now that everything has settled down after the promulgation of the *Jōyō Kanji* List (Tanaka 1991: 142). Certainly, with the present list functioning smoothly, there is as yet no real move within the Council to alter it, as was confirmed by an interview with a Council representative. Although word processing has spread more rapidly than was at first thought possible in the last ten years, there are still many people who either do not use it or are positively opposed to the idea. The English-language typewriter and later the computer encountered similar pockets of opposition when first introduced in the west, and yet today it is the norm to use them. It remains to be seen whether this technology will spread as far in Japan as its English-language equivalent has done overseas. If it does, and it seems highly likely that it will, then the Council is moving to face the challenge, although it is not yet clear what form the surveys and countermeasures referred to will take.

Regardless of personal taste in writing implements, nobody appears to dispute that the word processor will become a catalyst for change, removing as it has some of the rationales which underpin the present policy. The interim 1992 Council report recognised the validity of suggestions for change in the teaching mix of characters:

> 'The rapid development of electronics could not have been foreseen by earlier sessions of the Council. Writing characters (input) has become much simpler, and the ability to read them has become very important. We need to think carefully, in connection with the spread of the word processor, about the division between characters for recognition and those for reproduction, and about whether or not we should increase the number of characters people can read.' (Kokugo Shingikai 1992: 13)

If such an outcome were to eventuate, it would inevitably create a generation gap between pre- and post-policy-educated members of the community. Such a gap is not new to Japan, however, and need occasion no lasting concern. People educated prewar were used to a much wider range of characters, many of which had more complex shapes, and to a different method of kana spelling than those educated after the postwar reforms. The gradual spread of the reforms through the community in this case was facilitated by two things: their adoption in school textbooks and other government documents, and their voluntary implementation by the print media. My earlier book on script policy cites several major surveys on the effect of the new policies and the time which elapsed before they became entrenched. The general consensus was that while people over forty might have struggled with the modernised kana spelling, school students and teachers coped well and by the fifteen-year mark, the desired results were being achieved (Gottlieb 1995: 158–160).

The eventual outcome of this process will be of interest not only to the Japanese themselves but also to all those of us around the world who are either learning or teaching the language. Because of the push by the Japanese government to promote the teaching of Japanese overseas through the activities of the Japan Foundation, any change in the official script policy and its application in education will inevitably have a flow-on effect to hundreds of thousands of foreign learners as well as to the people of Japan itself. There has been for some years an ongoing debate in TJFL classrooms as to the best way of teaching characters: should they all be taught for both recognition and reproduction, which means that the number of characters which can be taught in the average degree span is limited by time constraints to about 1,200? Or should only a few hundred be taught for reproduction and much greater numbers than at present for recognition, so that our students' reading abilities are not constrained by the need to spend an equal amount of time learning to write characters which they may never need to use? The eventual outcome of the script policy debate occasioned by the word processor will thus reverberate widely through that part of the global community which is concerned with the Japanese language.

The long-term outlook

All in all, then, will the word processor change Japanese? Opinions vary. Kabashima Tadao has adopted a long-term evolutionary view, locating the word processor on a continuum of sweeping changes which have transformed the face of written Japanese over the last hundred years. These changes have included the development of a modern colloquial style to replace the archaic style in use well into the modern period (see Twine 1991); the postwar script reforms, in particular the character limits and the modernisation of kana spelling (see Gottlieb 1995); and the postwar influx of non-Chinese loanwords, which is even more marked today in the areas of computers and information processing. One cannot therefore evaluate whether the word processor will influence Japanese or not without considering the issue in the context of the great change from past to present and now to future, in which the word processor may be just one element. There will be no influence on grammar and phonology, but there will be a conservative influence on the lexicon, brought about by the preservation of Sino-Japanese words written in kanji. In addition, texts will become more visually interesting through the use of a wider range of fonts (Kabashima 1988: 25–27). In short, in this view, the changes to written Japanese will be mechanical rather than organic.

Kabashima's point deserves emphasis because it underlines the major shift in attitudes to writing which has occurred over the last hundred years. Whereas in the premodern and early modern period form was often regarded as being more important than content, in the information era it is the unfettered transmission of information which has become important. Along the way, as Kabashima rightly points out, various significant stylistic and orthographic reforms have been enacted without which such an outcome would not have been possible. It is therefore (probably) appropriate to view the word processor not as an overpowering agent of unexpected change but as just another link in a cycle of rationalisation which may not yet have run its course. To someone like Yamada Hisao, however, the cycle will not be over until romanisation has been achieved. To others, the next step might be the leap from keyboard input to voice synthesis. Whichever view one takes, however, it seems likely that the word processor will have a more substantial impact on written Japanese than the lexical conservatism and innovative formatting Kabashima predicts. As we have seen, available evidence indicates that there is indeed some degree of influence on orthographic choices as a whole.

A conservative influence in terms of maintaining the status quo has been predicted by Mita Masahiro: because it is not the word processor but the user who controls the input, there will be no change - the word processor will in fact prevent change in the written language because the inevitable timelag between the coining of a popular neologism and its appearance in a word processor's dictionary will mean that these words will not come into use in writing. In this sense - that the latest words will not be instantly available in the dictionary but will require the effort of extra keystrokes to input - the status quo will be maintained, as people tend to accept whatever the conversion process offers them first. Perhaps any change will be cultural rather than linguistic, with an increase in *minikomi* (mini-media, as opposed to *masukomi*, mass media) resulting from desktop publishing (Kida, Furuse et al. 1987: 169 and 182).

In Ogino's view, it is possible for language to be changed by developments in writing implements: script and writing implements have always been closely linked, like clay tablets and cuneiform or brushes and cursive writing. There is a distinction between *gengo taikei* (total language system) and *gengo kōdō* (language behaviour). The former transcends individual differences, is widely understood and therefore exists on the social level; the latter differs from person to person and therefore exists on the level of the individual. It is important to distinguish between the two when questioning whether the use of the word processor will bring about changes in the language. Indubitably language behaviour can be affected by the orthographic choices a writer makes, eg whether to write a word in kanji, hiragana or katakana. This sort of choice has nothing to do with the language system, as whichever way the word is written it is still Japanese. From the writer's point of view, however, the choice is important, as different orthographies project different nuances. If the word processor dictionary gives only the character and not the other two versions, the tendency to take whatever is first offered will increase the use of the character, thus affecting language behaviour. Perhaps in time, if a sufficient number of language behaviour changes of this sort accumulate, a change in the language system as well might eventually result, as the language system has certainly changed over the last few hundred years in Japan in a gradual process of evolution. Language change within the same era is perceived as being a matter of generational differences; the new usage of the younger generation is the forerunner of the next generation's standard usage. As changes in language behaviour could certainly therefore over time bring about a change in the language system, it is difficult to state categorically that the system will not eventually be changed by the word processor (Ogino 1990: 21–22).

Most of the opinions I have examined in this chapter were first presented several years ago. There seems more recently to be a slackening of debate on the issue, as if the first flush of examination of the new way of writing has worn off, although Ogino's research group continues with their work. Word processing technology is constantly developing. Just as Fujisaki warned back in 1984 that it was dangerous to theorise about the impact of the word processor on the language based on the machines which were then available (Fujisaki 1984: 114), so we would do well to keep that in mind today. As the initial problems are overcome, word processing ten years from now may present a very different aspect, particularly when voice recognition becomes a reality. The one refrain that remains constant has to do with the limitations of the dictionary. The size of the dictionary in terms of number of words remains a major selling point for different manufacturers, but the refining of the contents is not receiving proper attention. In Atsuji's opinion, it is the dictionary which will play a leading role in shaping the orthography in days to come, and dictionary-controlled Japanese will become the mainstream of the future (Atsuji 1991: 223).

Above all, it would seem that what is needed for an era when characters are handled electronically is standardisation of input, the *seishohō* referred to above by different writers and by the National Language Council, so that efficient searching of databases may be done and the computer, which has to be told exactly what to do, is clear on what form it is seeking. As we have seen, however, this idea has been met with resistance, on the grounds that it would lead to loss of individuality and to the loss of that prized diversity which has always been a feature of the Japanese script system. Since antiquity, notes Kabashima, the attitude of the Japanese has been to skilfully manage diversity and leave its regulation to chance. It was not until after the culture shock cause by contact with the west and later by the Occupation in particular that any attempt was made to seek orthographic uniformity. There were four different scripts, many kinds of premodern stylistic conventions and lexical diversity which saw both a Japanese word and a foreign loanword for, say, 'towel' (tenugui/taoru) in use at the same time. The increasing ability of word processors to handle a range of fonts and formats means that in mechanical terms they are becoming able to cultivate diversity and show nuances in a way attuned to Japanese tastes (Kabashima 1988: 28).

It is true that if a *seishohō* were in force the element of diversity would be somewhat constrained, insofar as it is possible for a script system which employs five (if the alphabet and Arabic numerals are included) different orthographic conventions ever to be constrained in terms of diversity. This certainly does not mean, however, that individuality of writing, which depends far less on orthography than on content, would be sacrificed as a result. What might be lost would be individuality of presentation, in terms of preferred use of *okurigana* and choice of script, but this can be more than compensated for in terms of the different fonts and other elements of presentation made possible by the word processor. Individuality of style, of course, as we shall see in the next chapter, is another matter altogether.

This chapter has examined the changes attributed to the word processor in the writing habits of its users. In a sense, this technology has brought about a major 'culture shock', to use a dated term: whereas in the west it evolved as the natural outcome of a long period of typewriter use, which accustomed people gradually to machine-produced documents, in Japan, because of the limitations earlier imposed by the script, everything happened within a period of a few years. This has naturally involved some changes to certain values and cultural practices as enculturation of the new technology proceeds. The following chapter will examine the social significance of the technology for its users.

Notes

1 A character usually has two or more readings (pronunciations). Its *on* (or 'Chinese') reading usually occurs when it is in a word of Chinese origin, whereas its *kun* (or 'Japanese') reading is assigned when it represents a native Japanese word. Since most Sino-Japanese words are compounds of two or more characters, most *on* readings occur in that context. When the character for 'shop' is used on its own to represent the Japanese word for 'shop', for example, it is pronounced 'mise' (*kun* reading); when it occurs in the word 'shop assistant' ('ten'in'), it is pronounced 'ten' (*on* reading).

2 The Showa Period is the name given to the reign of the last emperor (1926–1989).

CHAPTER FOUR

Some Cultural Consequences of the Technology

What are the cultural consequences of word processing technology for its users in Japan? This chapter will examine the social impact of the word processor on a range of accepted conventions, probing changes in the interface between writer and text and in the idea of writing as mediated by the new 'implement'. It will also examine the role of this particular example of new technology in identity construction: what image, if any, is the choice of a word processor as writing implement intended to project?

The twentieth century has seen important changes in Japanese orthography as a result of the script reforms discussed earlier. A further prominent feature has been the change from brush culture to pen culture and now to keyboard culture: in other words, a change from the 'hard' to the 'soft' era, with the accompanying social ripples each step creates. Such a transition has inevitably brought with it value judgements relating to each of the new writing implements as they appeared. Because the word processor is a machine at which one sits, not an implement which one holds in the hand, some ambiguity has surrounded the precise definition of its role in the writing process. As a result, a lively debate surrounds its enculturation, informed by deep-seated fears of the encroachment of technology into writing, one of the most personal of domains. We might profitably begin by examining attitudes to writing implements, in order to better understand the affective arguments which surround the word processor today.

In the era of brush and ink, some people considered it rude to write in ordinary ink rather than the traditional Japanese *sumi* ink, believing that to do so indicated insufficient respect towards the recipient. A letter written in *sumi* gave an impression of politeness on the part of the writer and demanded a reply of equivalent quality in terms of stationery and presentation. Today, however, letters are commonly written with ballpoint pens. Regardless of content, such letters may look cheap but convey the impression of a 'witty and unpretentious' writer. Letters in pencil, at the bottom of the hierarchy, are childish and naive (Horii 1990: 64).

The value hierarchy surrounding writing implements ranks brush, fountain pen, ballpoint pen and pencil in descending order. It is considered unacceptable to use a pencil for letters except in special circumstances. The 'fude-pen', a brush pen with built-in ink supply which became popular in the 1980s, ranks somewhere between one and three on this scale, with the word processor coming in between three and four. Fashions change: when people began writing with fountain pens in the Meiji Period it took about three years before invidious comparisons with the brush began to die down; much later, an article from the Asahi Shinbun described writing a letter to one's superior in ballpoint pen rather than fountain pen as a breach of respect. The fountain pen, which became the most respected writing implement after the brush, was replaced by the ballpoint pen because ballpoints are cheaper and do not require refilling: statistics from the 1987 Japan Industrial Yearbook indicated a more than 50% drop in production from 958,198 dozen fountain pens in 1980 to 442,799 dozen in 1985, compared with a rise in production for ballpoints from 419,922,000 to 433,345,000 for the same period. This blurring of values indicated by the decline in pre-eminence of the fountain pen made it likely that the word processor also had a chance of being accepted as an appropriate medium for correspondence (Yamaneki 1988: 93–94). Other figures reported in a 1991 Asahi Shinbun article indicated that even the ballpoint pen as well as the pencil in offices had by then been routed by the introduction of word processors. After 1984, the number of black pens used in various sections of the main Tokyo branch of the Asahi and in its other branches dropped by half; with articles increasingly being produced on word processor, this decline was expected to continue (no author given, 1991).

The personal letter

The development of new writing implements has therefore meant that earlier value judgements attached to particular writing implements have in turn been superseded as each new one becomes embedded in popular use and acceptance. As always, of course, there are those who remain wedded to the older forms, usually on the basis of some assigned moral superiority, as illustrated by the case of the brush in Japan and later the fountain pen. These judgements are suspended in the office domain, where it is considered appropriate that machines such as the typewriter or word processor be used for document production. When the new technology strays into the domain of the personal, however, feelings are apt to run high. In the case of the word processor in Japan, as with the typewriter in the west, the crux of the matter is the use of a machine to initiate or respond to personal contact rather than the human agency of the pen or brush. What effect does the use of machine-printed characters for such contact have on interpersonal relations?

Before we look at the debate on this matter, it would be instructive to consider the related debate as to whether the word processor is in fact a machine or a tool (*dōgu*). Is it the latest in a long line of writing implements, or is it a newfangled machine? One definition offered is that a machine is something which far exceeds the capabilities of a human being and has an aura of mystery about its workings for the ordinary person which inspires gratitude, whereas a tool helps with work but does not 'far exceed' the capacities of the user. The typewriter is definitely a tool in the common view. Which is the word processor? Is it just a typewriter with memory capacity and editing functions? On balance, no. With the typewriter, the user can clearly see the hammer jump up and hit the ribbon when the key is struck. With the word processor, there is no such visual evidence of how it works, so that the kanji conversion process (enabling the writing of characters in numbers far beyond the ability of a human user to recall) imparts the element of mystery characteristic of a machine. It is therefore definitely a machine, but the early days was used more as a tool, limited to making clean copy rather than expanding into the area of intellectual production (Nomura 1984: 16–17). Since then, of course, that desired amplification has taken place in no uncertain terms, and when the term 'tool' has been used in the literature, as it very frequently has over the last ten years, it has been in connection with user responsibility rather than with the nature of the technology itself.

The issue of whether the new technology is appropriate for use in personal communications has emerged as one of its main sites of confrontation. Many older people, in particular, feel affronted by the idea of receiving personal letters which are not handwritten. Quite apart from the appropriateness of such a letter within the social context, older people often complain that printed characters are somehow 'cold' and lack individuality, as was said of the first typewritten letters in other countries. On the other hand, this charge is brought against all new writing implements and should not be taken seriously; content is obviously more important in determining the tone of a text than form (Ogino 1987: 34). In Japan, where calligraphy is an art form and where judgements about character can be made on the basis of people's handwriting, it is only to be expected that this kind of emotional reaction will appear in the wake of a sustained attack on the dominance of handwriting such as the word processor presents.

Lingering in the background to the concern with printed letters is the suspicion that because documents can be saved in a word processor's memory a generic form letter for particular occasions could be composed and then called up and adjusted as appropriate when required. The result would lack the directness and personal touch of a freshly written letter aimed specifically at one recipient alone. Newspapers in the second half of the 1980s showed an increase in the number of letters from readers concerned at the perceived blandness and lack of warmth of letters written on word processors. It is the division between the social and the personal that is at issue here. When a letter is sent between two parts of the wider society (such as a letter from a company to a company) or from a social entity such as a company or government office to an individual, it is taken for granted that such communications will be printed and no criticism is forthcoming. It is also permissible for mass convention-dictated mailouts from an individual to society at large (as in the case of New Year greetings or other seasonal greetings) to be printed. The problem only arises in the case of a private one-off communication between two individuals, where multiple copies are not involved (Yamaneki 1988: 90–91).

Academic Morioka Kenji recounts the tale of his struggles to produce a postcard when he was first learning how to use his word processor in the early 1980s. Flushed with success, he sent it off, only to have it criticised by the recipient, who said that the printed postcard did not have a 'human familiarity' about it and that he would have preferred a handwritten one. Another letter he wrote to a young person earned a similar response, this time with the grumble that the recipient had thought it was a letter from the courts. Morioka had written with every intention of being polite, but apparently what was missing was the air of familiarity which handwriting conveyed. What surprised him was that these comments came not from older, more conservative types but from people only seventeen or eighteen years old. He nevertheless persisted in using his word processor for personal communications, believing that the extra information he could pack into a postcard because of the smallness of the print compensated for any impersonality because it then approximated the length of a letter, and allowed him to go into the sort of detail which handwriting would not allow in that limited space (Morioka 1984: 73–74).

To write a letter ('tegami o kaku') has now come to mean for many to type a letter ('tegami o utsu') on the word processor. To some, to answer a beautifully written *sumi* letter with a printed one would be insulting. One opposing view is that in this age of internationalisation, communication itself is prized about everything else, and clear communication is best suited by a practical format such as horizontally written letters rather than exquisite vertically-written brush formats on carefully chosen rice paper. Those who complain that the human factor is missing from printed characters are correct in a literal sense, in that it is possible to make certain limited value judgments about a person from their handwriting. If the characters are scribbled, you might imagine that they were written in a hurry, or that the writer was careless. Neat characters, on the other hand, might conjure up an impression of a careful or rather formal person. In that sense, the word processor does to an extent disguise personality and prevent these arbitrary value judgments based on handwriting, although of course it does not hide a writer's individual stylistic characteristics. Typed characters do lack the impression of tangible warmth generated by handwriting, however bad; nevertheless a writer's humanity and warmth shines through his or her writing style and personality may be intuited by reading between the lines (Horii 1990: 60–62).

Regardless of social disapproval from certain quarters, the use of the word processor for letters is bound to continue and to spread. In the view of one commentator late in the 1980s, people are writing significantly fewer letters not just because they are busy and have less time but also because they are often not familiar with the basics of how letters should be set out. Citing a book of language-related questions and answers published by the Agency for Cultural Affairs (a section of the

Education Ministry) which contains a section on letter writing, he reflected that a person unused to writing letters by hand would find it quite difficult to follow the rules it set down. Using a word processor to write letters allows the flexibility to rewrite parts where needed, making it easier to observe these conventions. If everybody used one, some psychological resistance arising from invidious comparisons with handwriting might continue for a while but eventually there would come a time when all letters would be printed, particularly given the big improvement in the functions on offer: a font which imitated brush style had been developed in order to try to overcome this charge of 'coldness' in letters. The dissemination of the postwar script reforms had shown the three things with the strongest influence on a change in writing behaviour to be government offices, schools and the mass media. If government offices, which in the late 1980s still favoured the use of the ballpoint pen, were to take a strong line in acknowledging documents produced on a word processor, then things would change rapidly, just as the 1908 removal of the ban on the use of ink in official government documents had contributed to the spread of the fountain pen and increased the production of paper (Yamaneki 1988: 91–93).

On the one side, then, the tradition and personality arguments; on the other, the convenience and contemporaneity counterarguments. Writers such as those cited above relate anecdotal evidence that printed letters are on the increase. Do these perceptions reflect widespread change? Without large-scale surveys of writing habits it is impossible to say with any degree of certainty. There have, however, been smaller surveys conducted which offer empirical data. One, for instance, surveyed 89 people in 1987 to try to determine whether word processor users feel differently about their language and writing habits. Forty-six percent of respondents indicated that they used the word processor for letters and postcards, the second most common use after advice notices and leaflets (54%) (Endō, Kuwabara et al. 1987: 118). A 1992 questionnaire with 687 respondents, all or them members of the Japan Information Processing Society, found that only 21.4% used the word processor for letters to friends. In letters to benefactors, this percentage was even less (15.2%). Considerations such as politeness and friendliness are thus clearly important in the area of personal letters. On the other hand, 39.5% of respondents used the word processor for New Year and other seasonal greetings, such as the traditional summer inquiries after a person's health, which are qualitatively different from personal letters. The fact that 20% of respondents use a word processor even for personal correspondence, though, marks a significant change. On the evolutionary continuum of writing implements, the word processor today is in the position of the fountain pen when letters were written with a brush, or later the ballpoint pen when letters were written with a fountain pen. These earlier implements were first used by pioneers; although initially this created a sense of dislocation from accepted norms, in time with more widespread use that resistance disappeared, and it is reasonable to assume that the same thing will happen with the word processor. Unexpectedly, this survey indicated that older people are more likely than younger to use it for personal letters - unexpectedly given that younger people often adjust more quickly to a new technology than their elders. This could be because young people, in particular women, strive to infuse their letters with individual and friendly touches such as little drawings and cute symbols, and these are easier to do by hand (Ogino 1994: 10).

Letter writing is in any case declining as communication habits change. A 1987 survey on lifestyles and communication which appeared in the Asahi Shinbun on July 10 found that many people used the telephone in preference to writing for non-business communications, and close to 60% of respondents wrote not so much as a single letter or postcard a month. As e-mail spreads and accelerates this trend in the future, it may well be that a personal letter written on paper will become a rarity, in which case it is will no longer matter whether the characters are printed or not.

The handwriting complex

Despite these arguments as to the validity of non-handwritten letters as a means of interpersonal communication, one of the most often-cited reasons why people gladly take to using a word processor is precisely because it releases them from their handwriting complex (eg Ogi 1984: 57, Toyota 1988: 1104, Tanaka 1991: 128–129, Andō 1988: 101, Mizoe 1982: 11 and many others). In other words, it is precisely because they do not wish to be judged on the basis of their handwriting that many people welcome the freedom and 'anonymity' of print. The character complex is said to be alive and well in Japan because in the so-called kanji culture countries of East Asia there exists a special concept of 'appreciation of beauty' in writing, along with an ethic which suggests that one can judge a person's education, personality and feelings from their writing (Tsuzugi 1984: 64). A set of values surrounding kanji has developed over their long history of use, so that in Japan the character itself becomes a literary work in the *shodō* (calligraphy) art form and people search for originality and character therein (Kida, Furuse et al. 1987: 56). Small wonder, then, if those brought up in this tradition feel less than willing to expose poor handwriting to the inspection of others.

For people concerned about their writing, the word processor is psychologically a liberating force, freeing them from bother and embarrassment (a view shared by many from other countries and other language groups as well). This has in turn had a flow-on effect in increasing the volume of printed material circulating in society: released from the tyranny of handwriting (or no longer able to use that excuse to avoid writing), more people are writing than before (Ishiwata 1988: 16). Forty-nine percent of the respondents to the first survey mentioned above indicated that they had become less anxious about writing (30%) or that it had become easier (19%); of these, 80% gave one of their reasons as being that they no longer had to worry about whether their handwriting was good or not (Endō, Kuwabara et al. 1987:

120). In the second survey, 216 of the 687 respondents indicated that they wrote more as a result of using a word processor, and 89 listed 'it gets rid of my handwriting complex' as one of the specific advantages (Ogino 1994: 106, 110). And in the small Atsuji survey referred to in Chapter Three, more than half those surveyed gave trouble with handwriting as their main motivation for learning to use a word processor (Atsuji 1991: 195–196).

The 'objectivity' of printed characters is often listed as one of the major reasons why a word processor is to be preferred to handwriting, along with its editing functions. Bad handwriting, whether caused by tiredness or sloppiness, can be disguised by characters that are machine-like in appearance, allowing the document to be judged on its own merits without affective judgments concerning character clouding its reception. Not only the reader but also the writer approaches the document more objectively, without the same sense of attachment to painstakingly produced handwritten characters, which makes it easier to edit without regrets. The word processor therefore facilitates a growth spurt in the ability to write documents once the labour of writing 'good' characters is removed (Tsuzugi 1984: 64–65). This implies a change in the sense of ownership of a text depending on the medium by which it is produced, as well as a change in the interface between writer and text and writer and the concept of writing itself as mediated by the new writing tool. The matter of the handwriting complex perhaps illustrates better than anything else the change from brush culture to pen culture to keyboard culture and the affective arguments that have attended the earlier stages in this continuum. With the shift from 'subjective' handwriting to 'objective' keyboard, the text becomes one step removed from the writer (although of course still stamped with his or her personality through choice of words and style). The sense of 'ownership', which at first glance might seem to be diluted by this means, is in fact strengthened, therefore, by the greater freedom the impersonality of the characters allows in the editing process.

Many writers confirm that they do indeed experience an increased perception of authorial distance when they use a word processor, a sense of freedom from the subjectivity which ownership of handwriting imposes. In other words, the negative element of the ownership of the material is removed when handwriting is removed. Journalist Tanaka Ryōta, for instance, regards a handwritten manuscript as the offspring or 'other self' of the writer. Because it is too familiar, it is hard to carry on an objective dialogue with it, as it were, and to fix imperfections. The same text produced on a word processor, although still written by the same person, seems more removed because the handwriting element has gone. It then becomes possible to deal with it coolly, in a detached manner (Tanaka 1991: 130–131). Author Miura Shumon agrees: when he sees his own writing in print, he feels somehow disconnected from it, as if it is not his and he can look at it objectively, whereas rereading his own handwritten text is like looking at his face in a mirror (Miura 1984: 70).

It is not only writing that is made easier, of course, but also reading. Where previously the reader might have struggled to decipher bad handwriting, now he or she can easily read the printed text, regardless of what affective judgements on the appropriateness of the medium might be held. Ogino predicted that the speed of reading would increase as handwriting was replaced with word processor printing, and that this could only be a good thing as information could then be more efficiently transmitted. In short, the word processor has brought about an increase in the amount of information circulating in society. The easier it is to write, the more is written; the easier it is to read, the more is read. The advent and widespread use of this technology has therefore greatly accelerated the information society (Ogino 1987: 34).

The written word – written how?

Quite apart from the consideration of bad handwriting, there has also been considerable debate on the general issue of handwriting versus word processing. Much of the discussion revolves around the central question of what constitutes writing now, in the electronic age. Does 'to write' (kaku) really now mean mostly 'to type' (utsu)?

The question of whether a word processor allows people to 'write' or not has been analysed in terms of the three main motivations for writing: expression (to express what is in one's heart), communication (to communicate it to others) and scrutiny (to see if what has been expressed and communicated is valid). What a word processor produces is a document for communication, certainly, but in one view this is communication to an amorphous 'everyone' rather than to a specific 'you'. It is impersonal, like a loudspeaker: when a writer creates a document on the word processor, his or her heart becomes the loudspeaker. With a word processor, everything becomes a matter of 'choice'. The writer 'selects' the characters and forms the sentences, then 'selects' the font and other formatting aspects for the completed document. Given the entirely deliberate nature of this process, there is no way in which the inner thoughts the writer wishes to express can emerge spontaneously. Instead of being as it were a shout from the whole body, the 'form' is chosen for ease of reading (Saeki 1987: 58). In other words, the nature of writing becomes more calculated, less spontaneous, and is ruled by considerations of the visual impact of the final form.

Characters, this analysis continues, reveal the flow of human actions known as 'writing'. Even badly written characters can sometimes be deciphered by trying to recreate the action of the hand to see how they were written. Through the way in which the characters are simplified in writing, the flow or the rhythm is communicated to the reader. Recent word processors have attempted to provide an equivalent for this with fonts that recreate cursive shapes, but these are not genuine 'written' things, they are mere imitations of writing. People today perhaps pretend, when they use these fonts, that they are 'writing from their hearts'. When writers fall into the trap of seeing all characters as no more than patterns which they can 'select', however, characters are relegated to the status of a fragmented array of fonts chosen on the basis of certain distinctive characteristics. It then becomes much harder to master the technique of clothing the meaning of words in a flow of natural human movement. The word processor is thus not suited to the first of the criteria for writing listed above, ie expression of what is in the heart. It does, however, fulfil the other two, in that it has the ability to communicate (in a loudspeaker fashion, rather than on a personal plane) and is excellent for the objective scrutiny of the appropriateness of what has been written. The three functions of writing will eventually lose their integrated relationship as technology develops new and more advanced writing implements; they will become independent of each other. The new definition of creativity and autonomy in writing will be found in how well a writer 'selects' and 'combines'.

When the technology first appeared, as we have seen, some were so entranced by its possibilities that they predicted the total disappearance of handwriting. With time and experience, however, such grandiose predictions settled down and are now seldom heard. And yet, concerns do remain. Coming back to the earlier analysis of the three component elements of writing as expression, communication and scrutiny: Saeki warns that the use of the word processor may eventually distort all three. Since its 'public' communication and 'public' scrutiny functions are increasing, one might easily think that all is now made convenient, efficiency has been improved and quality increased. However, the questions remain: has the introduction of the typewriter in the west led to the distortion of writing there? In the case of China and Japan, has the change in writing implements from brush to pen and then to pencil meant the 'corruption' of writing? Saeki himself believes this to be true, that the change in writing implements has meant a loss to culture of the richness of 'writing', and that therefore the things which people wrote in bygone days ought to be treasured as an important cultural inheritance from the days when writing really was writing (Saeki 1987: 59–60).

A 1989 article in the journal Da Capo showcased several writers who used word processors on a daily basis, reporting their views on what changes they thought the technology had brought about in the nature of writing in Japan. Had it improved composition? Did writing on a word processor have any special characteristics? Kida was one of those interviewed. He had begun using a word processor in his mid-40s, by which time his writing style was already established and was therefore not changed. He noted, however, that the essays of young people who used word processors favoured short sentences and were full of hiragana because the writers had skipped the bother of using the kanji conversion key. Kida likened this to what he described as the so-called 'hardboiled style with a sense of speed' which had appeared in the west when people moved from handwriting to typing. Editor Nemoto Masao agreed: younger writers, he found, were using a higher proportion of colloquial language in their writing. While word processors were not entirely responsible for this, there was no doubt that they were suited to that kind of style. Word processors also resulted in a much more polished finished product than formerly, because of the editing functions. Not all young writers were using word processors, however; Nemoto cited Shimada Masahiko and Yoshimoto Banana as two who continued to write by hand (various 1989: 21–22).

Several years earlier, it had been predicted that the word processor would bring about a revolution in writing because people who did not polish their work sufficiently when handwriting could now rely on the help of electronic editing, and since the word processor did the mechanical work of 'writing' in the sense that it printed out beautiful characters, the writer was therefore free to concentrate his or her energy on writing good text. In the Da Capo article, freelance travel writer Gotō Hiroshige reported that this had been exactly his experience. The ability to edit electronically had relieved much of the pressure he felt in writing; whereas with handwriting he was conscious of the need to craft the structure of a sentence before committing it to paper, with the word processor he was able to chop and change at will. Whether this resulted in better writing in the sense of superior text, of course, was open to debate. Some, such as author Miura Shumon, welcomed the fact that the word processor's on-screen editing had solved earlier problems of logical flow being obscured by changes made during handwritten editing. Others, such as Nishimura Hirohiko, cautioned that over-zealous use of the editing functions without due regard for continuity could result in disjointed text. The word processor and the xerox machine have between them changed the nature of the committee consultative process, Nishimura complained. All members of a committee read the first draft of any document and made some changes, which were then incorporated into the second version. Then everyone had a say in the polishing and a third draft was made. The final draft appeared when unanimous agreement was reached. One might think that these multiple inputs would eliminate all the defects and result in excellent text, but in fact they often resulted in illogical, poor writing which lacked the proper rhythm and flow. The more a document was changed, the less controlled and the worse it became (Nishimura 1986: 11).

Ogino's 1992 survey questioned respondents as to their perceptions of how their writing had changed with word processor use. The answers indicated that many people (279 out of 687) now began writing long articles not from the beginning, as when they wrote by hand, but from any place they wanted, adding bits in here and there as they went along. This trend would increase as word processor use spread, Ogino predicted. One of the other ways in which he thought style might be changing was that because the word processor was unsuited to the use of very colloquial expressions due to the time lapse between their appearance in society and their incorporation into word processor dictionaries, text was now being written very clearly, without contractions or omission of particles (Ogino 1994: 113). This is at odds with Nemoto's observation above that young writers were using more colloquialisms, but Ogino is referring to scientific writing rather than fiction. There is of course nothing stopping anyone from using colloquialisms in a word-processed article provided that they are willing to key in the extra strokes to produce them rather than rely on the dictionary to provide them. The putative nature of the style would therefore seem to be in the hands of the user, as always: those who are willing to take what the word processor throws up may appear to be heading towards a machine-controlled style, those who are willing to shape the machine to their own ends will retain their autonomy. This is also Ogino's conclusion as he reflects on the results of his survey. Because writing has become easier on account of the word processor, people now write much more; the word processor has made them 'dispatchers of information'. But it is after all only a tool, and the user controls what comes out of it.

The consensus on the suitability of the word processor to particular genres of writing appears from a study of the literature to be that it may most appropriately be used in genres which require carefully reasoned development of an argument rather than spontaneity of expression, provided that due attention is paid in the editing process to knitting together sections which may have been changed so that they form a seamless whole. One of the best and most representative discussions of this issue comes from a chapter in Tanaka's 1991 book *Wapuro ga Shakai o Kaeru* (The Word Processor will Change Society), which I summarise here. The chapter begins with an evaluation by several well-known novelists of the usefulness or otherwise of the word processor in the creative process. For Sono Ayako, the difference between handwritten work and wordprocessed work is like that between *sumie* (Japanese black and white ink painting) and oil painting. A ten-page short story, written on 400-character-to-the-page squared manuscript paper, must have the sharpness of a knife and can be written at one sitting. A longer story requires the technique of an oil painter: the longer one can polish it, the better. To Sono, writing on a word processor is like producing that oil painting; she reads her own work over and over, much more than she does when writing by hand, checking it word by word and changing the order here and there, constantly polishing and refining.

Komatsu Sakyō, however, uses the word processor only for essay-type writing, feeling that to use one for a novel would upset the rhythm of his thoughts during the rewriting stage. With handwritten work, the corrected and crossed out parts are still there in case a reading of the whole text prompts him to change his mind; with a word processor, the corrected sections are gone for good once deleted. When he read a novel written by a younger writer, he was able to tell it was written using a word processor because the sentences lacked the smoothness one normally expects and had lost their individuality.

One of Japan's best known (and most translated) writers, Abe Kōbo (1924–1993), made an early foray into writing fiction on the word processor: his 1984 novel *Hakobun Sakura Maru* was noted as a pioneer in this regard, though many writers have since followed his lead. In an interview in the Asahi Pasokon magazine in January 1991, Abe put forward his pragmatic view: 'a word processor or a fountain pen is, after all, just the means with which to write ... what readers read is the style which has been written, not the tools with which it was written nor the penmanship. The style is what comes from the author's heart and mind'.

Reflecting on these comments and on the nature of the writing implement best suited to fiction, Tanaka recalls that Hemingway's work was often described as 'typewriter literature', an expression which emphasised a strong dry style, quite different, he asserted, from what could have been written with a pen. Hemingway used the typewriter to record the emotions of the 'lost generation' in a spare, precise, disciplined style. What implement would Japanese authors choose to 'fling down' feelings as they wrote? Not the word processor, even though like the typewriter it has a keyboard. Surely it would be the pen. When one writes with a typewriter, just as with a pen, there is a limit to the amount of polishing which can be done. The only way to remake the original into a completely different form is to abandon it and start again. The typewriter and the pen therefore both belong to the world of diagrammatic characters (*zukei moji*), the word processor to the world of electronic characters. Perhaps because of this difference in the nature of the typewriter and the word processor, writers and critics do not consider 'word processor literature' analogous to 'typewriter literature'. Indeed, it is not possible to have a 'word processor literature' in the sense of a style with the same characteristics across writers, since those who use the word processor to write do so in different ways which reflect their own approach to style: Mita, for instance, uses the editing function mainly to add to what he has already written, whereas Abe used it mainly to delete unwanted sections.

Tanaka's conclusion is that the word processor is really more of a tool for older writers of fiction, who construct their mature writing carefully and diligently, rather than for younger writers who write with more dash and zest and therefore still prefer to use a pen. In the non-fiction writing world, however, where the novelty of the writing is not considered as important, those such as academics, researchers, critics and journalists who write for a living have adopted the word processor wholeheartedly. By the end of the 1980s, a journal editor noted that every single manuscript submitted by researchers in their 30s was produced on word processor. With time, Tanaka predicts, this will become 'all those in their 40s' and eventually, regardless of age, just 'all'. Because the nature of the writing done outside the literary world is evaluated not on novelty or creativity but on such criteria as soundness of the data, strength of theoretical argument and clarity of argument in general, authors interested in developing this style of logical writing will naturally gravitate to the word processor, which allows repeated polishing of the text. In literature too much polishing can result in the loss of the text's original peculiar charm, but in other fields polishing is seen as an unconditional plus (Tanaka 1991: 120–125).

The description of the 'hardboiled' style produced by typewriter use is interesting. Kida Jun'ichirō is another who comments on it. Like Tanaka, Kida believes that established users who have set ideas about style and writing will find the word processor useful for producing structured, meticulous writing, although of course that does no more than build on abilities they already possess. For younger people of as yet unfixed writing habits, however, Kida believes that the word processor will bring about the same sort of cultural impact which was experienced in the early twentieth century in America when the 'hardboiled' typewriter style began to spread. By this he appears to mean a pared-down no-frills kind of writing, which is already visible in e-mail messages which feature abbreviated expressions and a particular special usage of their own. Young people who are inexperienced in writing adopt these conventions when they use the word processor and neglect the kanji conversion function, making do with hiragana where they really should convert to characters. To Kida, this is like making do with a nearby fast food outlet rather than going to the bother of crossing the road to reach the excellent restaurant on the other side. If this were to become entrenched as a convenience, he fears that it will become a universal cultural phenomenon in the future (Kida 1991: 52–53).

One important aspect of non-fiction writing, as opposed to fiction where there is usually a sole author, is the increasingly public nature of the writing process which the word processor has enabled. In academic writing, it is common for drafts of papers to be circulated for comment from colleagues, or to receive feedback after presentation at conferences, which is then incorporated into the text where appropriate. When the article is already held on disk in a word processor, of course, the process is much easier than if the whole thing has to be written out again by hand. In a sense, this knowledge that such work is going to be offered for the scrutiny of others involves a subtle shift in the nature of the writing process itself, which is no longer something private to the writer, written in the first instance for his or her eyes alone, but becomes something written from the very first draft for an 'other'. It is this change from private to public writing which Ogino believes will require standardisation in various areas: as the electronic handling of documents becomes more common, a document will have several owners. Of the 687 respondents to his questionnaire, 574 gave as one of the advantages of using a word processor the ability to revise documents easily, and 419 gave the ability to create a second document from one stored in memory. These two responses are closely linked, Ogino notes, and are related as well to the type of job that respondents (all of whom were researchers involved in some way in information processing) had. Research articles and conference papers are commonly rewritten many times; conference papers, once given, are usually rewritten and submitted to a journal (Ogino 1994: 107, 113). The kind of standardisation which Ogino envisions involves a greater precision in language use (because everything which a computer is to handle has to be clearly specified and available in the dictionary) and a flattening of demand for special types of orthography as generalist users accept what the computer already has on offer rather than go to the expense of adding specialist options (Ogino 1987: 64).

What the word processor has actually brought about, then, is a change in the concept of how one writes. Writing used to equate to filling in the holes on squared white manuscript paper (*genkō yōshi*) in a formalised, private process of committing thought to paper where one began at the beginning and went on to the end and where the actual shape of one's characters was cause for either pride or shame. Now that process is being replaced by a much less formal, less structured mode of arriving at the final product which often contains input from others, and where the physical manifestation of handwriting is no longer an issue. The fun aspects of this mode may contribute significantly to the future establishment of a grounded 'word processor culture'. Children in upper primary school enjoy the task of using a word processor to write, edit and produce a school newspaper, sharing different roles around in turn, and turning the writing assignment into an enjoyable process. If adults were to derive a similar pleasure from the process, that might well prove to be the face of the future (Mori, Yamane et al. 1988: 20–21). Certainly, one of the pleasures of writing with a word processor is the freedom to experiment with layout and font and to invest otherwise bland documents with 'personality' by this means. To many people, particularly younger users, this freedom equates to creativity in a visual sense, harking back to Saeki's comments about 'selecting' rather than writing being the defining criterion for quality of writing in the future. If layout and presentation assume an even greater importance than they hold today, then the word processor's dominance as the writing implement of choice would seem assured. The word processor, in the words of one article, 'by midwifing an interface between the computer and natural language, creates a space where we want to play a while' (no author given, 1996: 26).

The word processor may be said to represent an acceptable face of technology in an age where many perceive technological developments as an enemy resulting in redundancies and uncertainty for the work force. It is an acceptable face because it reinforces cultural norms surrounding script, puts Japan on a (relatively) equal footing with the west insofar as it allows electronic handling of characters, and involves no dirt or danger for the user. Strathern asks what kind of persons people are making of themselves out of using technologies pressed into cultural and social service 'which have material effects on the user of space, perceptions of time and so forth: however active the mind that socializes with the keyboard, the body is tied to a chair'. Part of the answer, she essays, is that users of domestic/communication technologies become empowered or enabled, that these technologies 'appear to amplify people's experiences, options, choices' (Strathern 1992: x–xi). Despite affective concerns surrounding script issues and interpersonal relationships, the word processor in Japan is certainly perceived on balance as an empowering force, enabling at last a certain degree of freedom in relation to the restrictions imposed by Japan's writing system, and having the potential to bring about a change in the national attitude to characters in the next century.

Some lifestyle consequences for the user

As we have seen, the cultural context for the word processor began to extend and diversify widely outside offices into homes, universities and research offices after 1982, when falling prices made its purchase a realistic option for individual users. The 1990 *Kokumin Seikatsu Hakusho* (White Paper on Living Conditions) provides tables showing the appearance of 8-bit word processors in households from 1981 and LCD word processors in households from 1984. The dissemination of personal computers began with the sales of 8-bit PCs in 1972, increased after the appearance of the much more efficient 16-bit PC in 1981 and passed 10% in 1989 as multi-function PCs became cheaper and smaller (Keizai Kikakuchō 1990: 173). After 1982, the White Paper tells us, many households bought word processors in order to create, store and save household documents, and also to use for New Year and other seasonal postcards and to store data such as address lists. The main objective of household information technology devices is to save labour, time and space: the word processor contributes in all three of these aspects in the home, with large amounts of information able to be stored comparatively rapidly and easily within one small word processor rather than on large amounts of paper requiring storage space. Portability, too, is an attractive aspect, particularly as stand-alone models have inbuilt printers and can be transported in cases no larger than a large shoulder bag or document case. And of course, as well as the system itself, the information it is used to produce is completely portable, as many people now walk around with floppy disks in their pocket, handbag or briefcase.

The information provided in the White Paper further indicates that the dissemination rate of compact disk players, word processors and personal computers was highest among those in their forties and fifties: 25–30% of people between the ages of 45 and 55 had a word processor, ie one person in four (Keizai Kikakuchō 1990: 189). This presumably reflects the fact of greater affluence among those with established careers. However, despite this high rate of ownership, the survey found that only about half the owners actively used the machines. Middle-aged people in their thirties and forties indicated intention to purchase when the price dropped further. In general, the desire to own a word processor increased when people reached the stage of using one at work. Few older people, however, had any interest in word processors or personal computers despite their clear benefits. Reasons given were that such machines were hard to use, that their display screens were too small to see clearly, and that using them would involve learning new skills. The White Paper indicated that there was a need to develop more user-friendly devices and to convince elderly people of the benefits of the technology so that they were not left out. This brings to mind the advertisements screened on Australian television in 1996 in which grandfathers communicated with distant grandchildren through e-mail and surfed the Internet, enthusing 'It's a wonderful time to be alive!' Such advertisements betoken a recognition of the need, in other parts of the world as well as Japan, to make the reach of the technology inclusive as the population ages.

As early as 1984, the word *waapurohorikku,* a pun on "workaholic" indicating a person who was forever in front of a word processor (*waapuro*), began to appear. These people, whose numbers were on the increase, were not just younger people who could come easily to grips with new technology or women whose jobs required them to use a word processor. The phenomenon was spreading among middle-aged men and also among people working in the humanities, who were usually considered less adept at adapting to technological innovation. In the not too distant future, it was predicted, there would be a word processor in every house, as Japan moved from 'the age of economics' to 'the age of culture' which the new machine suited so well (Tsuzugi 1984: 62–63). This scenario has not yet eventuated, but, as the figures in earlier chapters indicate, the rate of dissemination in private households has continued to increase.

Morioka Kenji had become such a *waapuro ningen* (word processor person, sometimes also referred to in the literature as a *kiibōdo ningen*, or keyboard person, meaning someone who hardly ever writes by hand) as early as 1984. By then he was writing all his manuscripts and personal communications on the word processor, and claimed to write nothing by hand. (Presumably by 'nothing' he means 'nothing substantial' – it is unlikely that, say, telephone messages would not be scribbled down by hand.) The cleanliness of the process attracted him: no longer did he have to endure the spectacle of eraser shavings covering the top of his desk as with a pencil, or stained fingers as with a pen. Thirty minutes of handwriting, Morioka recalled, and he would go to the garden to water the flowers, or read a book, anything for a change of pace. The word processor freed him to such an extent that he could now concentrate for two to three hours at a time, so that he wondered how much greater his productivity might have been if this technology had been available from his youth. Thanks to on-screen editing, word processing allowed him to arrive at the finished product much more quickly than handwriting, which wasted more paper with each fresh draft. He had often missed deadlines with his editor before because of the time needed for rewrites (Morioka 1984: 73–4).

Despite the advantages extolled by 'keyboard persons' such as Morioka and writer Sono Ayako, who related in 1985 that she was no longer happy writing by hand, education researcher Andō Shūhei warned people against becoming so dependent on the word processor that they felt unable to write without one. This he listed as one of the machine's disadvantages. Another was the possibility that spoken-language expressions might replace more formal written expression in text; people often become more verbose and chatty in word-processed communications. On the other hand, it is also possible to call up set phrases and assemble them as needed, with very little personal input at all. This could lead to formulaic writing, again undesirable. Word processor users should take care to write on a personal plane, while at the same time guarding against an inappropriate lack of formal written expression (Andō 1988: 102). One only has to consider the nature of most e-mail postings, which are chatty and often less formal than a letter might be, to understand what Andō is referring to, although his comments refer not to e-mail but to more general printed texts. Japanese has particularly strong conventions relating to the written language. With the Japanese typewriter, the time lapse between the original writing and the production of the printed clean copy left time for reflection on the form of the message. Word processing, however, with its instant printing facility, has closed that gap, not so much in the case of formal documents such as business documents or academic articles which are likely to be edited before printing but in one-off communications of a temporary nature. The flip side of using a word processor, however, as Andō warns, is its potential for producing formulaic communications using standard written language expressions called up from its memory, with the attendant danger that lazy users may over-rely on these and fail to inject the personal touch. Either way, this technology should be handled with care, and Andō viewed the rise of the *waapuro ningen* as a potential disaster.

Both the appearance of *waapuro ningen* and the increase in more moderate users have much to do with considerations of time, space, and economy, as well as being linked to aspects of identity creation through consumerism. Above all, the concept of convenience has played a substantial part. A 1983 report on the social impact of electronics was already describing Japanese culture as growing out of lives in which convenience was central, which would continue to seek a culture of comfort (Sōgō Kenkyū Kaihatsu Kikō 1983: 108). Convenience, as the *White Paper on Living Conditions* tells us, is the primary reason why the entry of the microcomputer into household appliances (which may now be extended to include the word processor) has changed people's lives, making them easier (Keizai Kikakuchō 1990: 175). In a sense it is ironic that convenience is advertised as one of the great virtues of the word processor, given that this technology makes available vast numbers of characters: in the script policy debates, it was the concept of convenience when related to script which came under vitriolic attack from conservatives and which was so strongly advocated by those who eventually succeeded in bringing about those postwar script reforms which word processing now appears to have gone so far towards overturning.

Convenience, however, is not always perceived as an unalloyed blessing. While the ease of input, editing and output the word processor offers is undeniable, we have already seen in earlier chapters that the convenience of accepting the orthographic choices first offered by the internal dictionary does not always produce desirable results. If 'convenient' simply stops at being 'easy', some felt, culture will inevitably decline as a result. To connive at turning out verbose, meaningless text just because it is easy to do is not acceptable. People must take pains to work out how best to use the word processor, which as an aid to composition is no more than a high-class tool, although just how 'high-class' is a moot point (Mizutani 1982: 25). Convenience, then, has hidden dangers and should be handled thoughtfully, with care.

In the home and the study, as well as in the office, word processing greatly reduces the labour and the time involved in document production. The space required for storage of documents is reduced because they are kept on disk; there is less paper rubbish produced in the draft stages of a document, and when the time comes to delete documents this can be done electronically without producing waste paper. Space considerations are particularly important in Japan, given the size of living quarters, and compact stand-alone word processors which incorporate their own printer are suited to such conditions. The issue of size has been important to the spread of word processors into homes, just as fountain pens, having been introduced during the Russo-Japanese war of 1904–05 when they were supplied to soldiers, began to spread into general use after that war because they could fit into the pocket of a suit (Yamaneki 1988: 95). One interesting sidelight worth mentioning with regard to space and economy is the setting up of at least three *waapuro kissaten* (word processor cafes) in Tokyo in the mid 1980s, much like today's Internet cafes. At *waapuro kissaten*, people could use a word processor for a while, either as a test run for intending buyers, or, for those who did not have the space or the money for their own, to process a document.

Of course, too much involvement with information technology can result in loss of space in the home as well: Kumon Shunpei of the International University of Japan's Centre for Global Communications (GLOCOM), for instance, relates that in the 1980s his life was revolutionised by the new media, with the result that his study, which used to contain just a desk and a bookcase, is now home to a personal computer, a word processor, a copier and a fax machine, which take up all the available space. He also owns a laptop, so that when he is out he can freely make memos and notes of meetings and so on. Like Morioka Kenji, Kumon writes everything from manuscripts to memos on these machines. He uses the word processor for his diary, and puts into personal databases details of important business cards and books that he might want to retrieve later. A new daily task for him then became to transfer what he did on the laptop when he was out onto his desktop word processor, for convenience of editing and printing (Kumon 1986: 63). This is perhaps an example of the two benefits of time and space savings being turned back on themselves, the space in Kumon's study having been colonised by the machines and the convenience of the technology having given rise to extra work of a different sort in the management of its various manifestations. Or perhaps it is not extra work, just a different kind of work. And in fact this incorporation of the technology into his daily routine indicates that it has in his case become fully functional, for as Silverstone reminds us, 'to become functional a technology has to find a place within the moral economy of the household, specifically in terms of its incorporation into the routines of daily life' (Silverstone, Hirsch et al. 1992: 24).

Despite the space advantages of disks, where several hundred documents could be stored on one floppy, Ogino's 1992 survey found that most people still preferred paper. When the 687 respondents were asked whether they would prefer to receive letters and documents on floppy disk or in hard copy, 147 of those who answered this question specified floppy and 353 paper. The reasons given for preferring floppies were that they made information easy to save and copy, that they could be added to as desired, that they were compact, that they could be easily searched, that they produced no rubbish, that they were light and that they were easy to read. Those who preferred paper did so because it could be read anywhere (ie without needing a machine), that it was easier to read, that it remained as a permanent record, that it did not strain the eyes, and that it was safer in case of accident. Paper was therefore still the medium of choice by a large margin. Those who preferred floppies tended to be researchers and younger people (Ogino 1994: 109).

The cost of paper is often mentioned as a saving when using the word processor, and can be offset against the cost of the machines themselves. Fukaya Tetsu, a lecturer at Osaka University, for instance, found writing by hand uneconomical because halfway through he would become selfconscious about his bad handwriting and the manuscript would end up in the waste paper basket. Or, if he picked up a started manuscript, he would want to make changes which would mean rewriting the lot; to write a manuscript of just a few pages therefore required a great deal of manuscript paper. Once he discovered the word processor, however, this waste became a thing of the past. No longer did he have to worry about bad handwriting, and as a result all his writing was now done on the new machine, which he had come to feel he could not write without (Fukaya 1984: 68). Quite apart from the expense aspect, which of course has to be balanced against the cost of floppy disks and electricity, the word processor/ personal computer is in this sense a 'green' technology, saving paper, providing of course that it is not just used as a clean copy machine for handwritten manuscripts and that editing is done on-screen.

There are of course some physical consequences to the user of adopting the new technology. Word processing has been cited as a source of stress, on account of worry over whether or not the user has chosen the correct characters from the alternatives suggested by the conversion process; of eyestrain; and of fatigue. The degree to which sitting typing at a word processor or personal computer causes fatigue or eyestrain has been the subject of some discussion, just as it has in the west. As far back as 1982, an Asahi Journal article warned that the early CRT screens, which could best handle characters, could lead to word processor-related health problems in the workplace and called for the development of liquid crystal displays which were less hard on the eyes (Iida 1982: 17). Since then, the consensus has been that two hours is the optimum length of a session; longer than that and frequent breaks should be taken. For those who use the word processor in private capacities, this may not be a problem, although care has to be taken not to forget the time when concentrating intensely. It is those who spend long hours at work who need to be particularly careful. Some academics (eg Fukaya, 1984) have found that injudicious over-exposure can result in eyestrain; others, such as Morioka Kenji, report no problem. The NHK television program referred to in Chapter Three, in which comparisons were carried out between word processors and handwriting, measured the amount of tear fluid in the eyes of two cohorts of writers, one of which was writing by hand and the other using word processors. There was no particular change over a 90 minute period in the fluid in the eyes of those who were writing by hand, but a noticeable drop in those who were not. Furthermore, those using the word processor blinked only 12 times per minute, as opposed to 28 times per minute for the others, prompting the program's presenter to warn word processor users of the dangers of 'dry eye', which could be prevented by conscious blinking.

The program further measured shoulder strain and finger fatigue, reporting that while shoulder strain was more pronounced among word processor users, handwriting produced much greater tension in the fingers and wrist. Many people have commented on the release from the physical fatigue of handwriting that the word processor has offered them. Sakamoto, for example, hailed the advent of the word processor with relief: as one who had taken shorthand in the Diet for thirty years, he was well acquainted with the cruel physical demands imposed by writing by hand, a labour which he described as exhausting the whole body (Sakamoto 1984: 62). Similarly, academic Kabashima Tadao has often recounted his difficulties with painful shoulders and hands brought on by writing by hand. When he spent all day writing a manuscript, the next day his shoulders would be so sore he could not work (Kabashima, Ichikawa et. al. 1987: 6). And Mizoe Masamichi, a member of the Asahi Shinbun's editorial staff, related that his bad habit of pressing too hard on his pencil invariably resulted in physical fatigue, which led him to purchase first a hiragana typewriter and later a word processor (Mizoe 1982: 11). These are not isolated instances (nor of course are they confined to the Japanese experience). For people such as the three just cited, the keyboard represents liberation from the physical tyranny of the pen. Given that the keyboard of the word processor or computer is much easier on the fingers, arms and shoulders than that of the earlier typewriters, it also represents a big step away from the physical duress involved in producing documents on those machines.

Consumerism

What of the place of the word processor in the consumer profile? In the 1980s, the word processor became an icon of chic as consumer fever swept the country. It became a symbol of the information society, marking its owner as a citizen of the information age as the technology was appropriated by the wider community. By 1988, Toyota Shigeo, an irritated supporter of kana, was able to remark that such was the brouhaha since the price had come down to the level at which even a 'salaryman' was able to afford one, that possession had become a matter of 'keeping up with the Jones' (or maybe the Tanakas). A word processor in the lounge room became the centre of a happy home, one of those accessories indicating a cultured lifestyle of which the owner could boast. The average family, remarked Toyota wryly, would not normally have a lot of things to produce on a word processor which could not be done with a pen – it was simply the 'in thing' to have letters printed out (Toyota 1988: 1104). To own a word processor, proclaimed the advertisements, stamped one as progressive, trendy, and in the know. It seemed 'advanced' to use such a machine.

The extent to which advertising images figure in the construction of identity through consumption is a matter for debate, and it may be too simplistic to assume that buyers seek to adopt the identities portrayed in advertisements. If the rate at which sales increased can be attributed in part to the influence of the kind of advertising described above, however, then in a sense word processor owners in the 1980s were constructing an identity as people in the vanguard of technology, unafraid of its demands, able to break free of the well-known 'keyboard allergy' of the Japanese and establish control of the new. They were active rather than passive consumers, eagerly seeking the new in order to deploy it to their own ends and to construct a social image of themselves in others' eyes. As Campbell writes, 'the consumption pattern that (individuals) select, whether represented by their choice of car or clothes, house, furnishings or leisure-time pursuits, can ... be regarded as indicative not simply of their 'self-identity', but of how they wish others to regard them' (Campbell 1995: 112). The link between consumer and observer in this nexus, however, as Campbell points out, is problematic, as the observer may not interpret the intended message as the consumer desires.

In a discussion of the larger sweep of domestic and communication technologies, Strathern writes: 'technology does not mediate the individual person's relationships with society; it has come to mirror the individual person's *consumption* of society' (Strathern 1992: xii). In the case of the word processor in Japan, both these descriptions are true. To a certain extent, as we have seen, an individual's relationships with society in the area of personal communications *are* being mediated by the decision to use print instead of handwriting, depending on the attitudes of both sender and recipient. At the same time, those who in the early stages in particular flocked to buy a word processor were to a certain extent signalling a consumption of society in terms of a willingness to break with accepted norms and subordinate sociability to individual desire. When this particular form of information technology entered households, it provided 'a means both for the integration of the household into the consumer culture of modern society – into a national as well as an international culture – and for the assertion of an individual's, a household's ... own identity: a domestic as well as a local culture' (Silverstone and Hirsch 1992: 4).

Word processor advertisements over the last few years have featured a multiplicity of ways in which the machines can be used to enhance the lives of the purchasers, ranging from business presentations to golf certificates to press releases, news letters, daily schedules, notices of all kinds and of course a bewildering range of postcard formats. One brochure, for Toshiba's Rupo JW88FX, congratulates purchasers on their cleverness, describing buying a word processor as investing in themselves. Different advertising discourses offer different user identities: a 1995 Toshiba Rupo JW-V600 brochure shows four different types of professional user ranging from corporate types to a female chef requiring printed menus, while a Casio Darwin G-770ZX brochure from the same year features an older man sitting in a home library and a younger woman in her lounge room. A 1996 brochure for the Casio Darwin G-900ST features an older professorial type and displays shots of the word processor among what are clearly meant to be scholarly surroundings. Jackson and Thrift, in their discussion of the geographies of consumption, neatly describe what is happening here:

> Within consumption studies, a useful starting-point is the suggestion that our identities are affirmed and contested through specific acts of consumption: we define ourselves by what we buy and by the meaning that we give to the goods and services that we acquire. But there is no essential, one-to-one, correspondence between particular commodities and particular identities: the same commodity can have radically different meanings for different individuals and for the same individual over time. Advertising and marketing campaigns have begun to realise this in targeting their products to specific niches. But rather than targeting particular market segments by associating their product uniquely and unambiguously with a particular lifestyle, they are increasingly trying to position their products in order to take advantage of the ambiguous and shifting boundaries of people's identities. (Jackson and Thrift 1995: 227)

Is consumerism a social force that maintains the status quo and encourages sameness? Or is it dynamic, allowing more assertion of individuality, singling people out from the crowd rather than making them part of it? At this stage of word processing's history in Japan advertisements would appear to be addressing more the second role, although at the same time insinuating that the first is the desirable end state in terms of the possession of the technology. It is not the possession of a word processor or PC in itself these days which bestows prestige but the variety of functions which it can undertake and the excellence of particular features such as printing or compatibility with Windows. The focus of the advertising may be seen as consumerism that allows control over one's own life, specifically over the construction of an orthographic identity. And of course this sort of consumerism implies a two-way dialogue with producers, as consumers indicate just what it is they seek and what they will or will not buy.

Sociologist Sugimoto Yoshio, discussing the argument advanced by many that Japan is a postmodern society, points out that two of the more heavily emphasised aspects in the Japanese context are the information revolution and consumerism. The information revolution thesis posits that the transfer of information has suddenly replaced the transfer of manufactured goods as the defining feature of contemporary Japanese society. Sugimoto outlines media critic Kogawa Tetsuo's argument that contemporary Japan is shifting from monetary capitalism to information capitalism as follows:

> The Japanese are now supposed to live in the most advanced information environment, which is dominated by such electronic devices as car telephones, vending machines for food and tickets, satellite and cable television networks, compact disk stereos, fax machines and word-processors. With Japanese electronics companies dominating both international and domestic markets, the Japanese life-styles are increasingly automated,

> their social relations are influenced by electronic media, and their mass culture presents itself through the medium of electronic devices.

On the consumerism argument for the post-modern theory, Sugimoto cites sociologist Imade Takatoshi, who argues that 'what drives the post-modernist Japanese is not the 'deprivation motive' with which people work to free themselves from economic hardship. Instead, the predominant force in post-modern society is the 'differentiation motive,' which prompts them to purchase luxury goods and services that would give them a sense of being different and distinguished from other people.' In this sense, Sugimoto continues:

> Japan has allegedly attained a level beyond the most advanced stage of western-style development, such as David Riesman's 'other-directed' type society and Walt Rostow's 'high consumer society', in which consumer conformism has dominated. In post-modern Japan, it is argued, consumer preference is diversified, and the distribution market is 'segmentalized' in such a way that a wide range of individual consumer choices can be met. Thus, the argument goes, Japan's commercial market cannot ignore, and in fact must calculate carefully, spenders' specific predilections for high-brand commodities, lavish services, and extravagant entertainments. Consumer conformity in modern Japan has been transformed into consumer diversity in post-modern Japan. (Sugimoto 1996: 145)

It is not the intention of the present book to argue whether Japan is a post-modern society or not. What is interesting in the context of an examination of the impact of word processing technology, however, is to note that in both the arguments advanced above, this technology plays an important role. The stand-alone word processor and the personal computer with its software package, as we have seen, play their parts in the increasing automation of Japanese life-styles, with some people depending on them for diaries, memos, schedules, postcards, even no doubt shopping lists. The gradually increasing acceptance of word-processed letters in lieu of personal handwritten communications as a viable social activity is a good example of social relations being influenced by electronic media. And the consumerism theory is amply borne out by looking at the differentiation between different models of word processor, each with its carefully guarded secrets of dictionary contents, each trumpeting aspects of (sometimes minuscule) difference in order to convince the discerning consumer, who wants above all to be different, to part with his or her yen. The word processor market exemplifies this catering on the part of producers to the consumers' desire for diversity. If, as Clammer has argued, contemporary Japanese consumption represents a kind of trying on of different models of society (Jackson and Thrift 1995: 222), then the case study of the word processor market reveals a social model delighting in diversity.

In practice, were the consumers themselves satisfied with their latest acquisition? Kuwabara's 1987 survey provides some fragmentary answers on this score. The 89 respondents were questioned as to how satisfied they were, overall, with their purchase. Not all answered this question, but of those who did, 44% professed themselves happy, and commented that the functions on their particular model were appropriate for the price paid, while another 19% replied that they were happy with the functions if not with the price (Endō, Kuwabara et al. 1987: 120). Satisfied purchasers outnumbered those with complaints, and what complaints there were related to the range of things that the machine could do, which may reflect unrealistic expectations in the first place. Certainly for many in the 1980s the word processor was seen as some sort of magic machine possessed of an inherent and mysterious 'creativity'. Poet Shimizu Tetsuo describes this belief as a modern myth, recalling that when he first began using a word processor in the early 1980s he had quite often been asked with wonderment whether the machine was capable of writing poetry. It was as if the machine were being treated as possessing some sort of magic power different from a fountain pen or a pencil, as if it were an 'automatic writing machine'. People need to realise, Shimizu warned, that the word processor is no more than a tool, that it only seems 'creative' or 'expressive' because of the variety of 'form' which may be achieved through the use of different fonts, lines and symbols (Shimizu 1988: 19). When buyers were faced with the reality that it is the user who creates and the machine that carries out the commands, disappointment may have set in on this account.

A further question sought information on what users found inconvenient, if anything, about their word processors. Here there was a clear majority who did have something to complain about: 77% found some aspects awkward, mainly to do with problems with the dictionaries (wrong conversions, lack of desired kanji). Only a minuscule 1% found nothing particularly inconvenient about the dictionary. The sorts of problems which arise with the dictionary have already been discussed in earlier chapters; this survey bears out the general consumer dissatisfaction with the performance of the dictionary regardless of the manufacturer. The survey was carried out in 1987, though, the year that artificial intelligence was introduced to dictionaries; things have no doubt improved since then. The standout responses on the other aspects of the word processor are the lack of compatibility with other machines (something which has since been rectified), the difficulty of understanding the manual and the inability to preview vertical written texts on screen.

Another general source of dissatisfaction was the rapid obsolescence of machines: the models changed so often that what had been bought was soon out of date. Several respondents suggested that old models should be traded in on newer versions at a discount, like cars, so that people could upgrade cheaply. Taken over all, Kuwabara reflected, while manufacturers were falling over themselves to improve their product, the aim of making the improvements was to differentiate their machines from those of other makers and to improve sales, not to increase the convenience of the machine for the purchaser. If manufacturers were really concerned about what their customers wanted, they would take into account such issues as compatibility between machines and upgrade facilities (Endō, Kuwabara et al. 1987: 125–126).

Many of the large number of articles on word processors and word processing published during the 1980s, particularly during the second half of the decade, contained warnings to potential buyers not to be dazzled by the new technology into buying something they did not really need but to think carefully about what it was they wanted the machine to do and to buy on that basis. Intending customers were advised to visit showrooms and *waapuro kissaten* to try out machines and to familiarise themselves with what was on offer. It was considered particularly important to do this given that the contents of the dictionary and the details of the kanji conversion process in each machine were usually industrial secrets, not made public for consumer perusal. While a manufacturer's catalogue might brag of the number of kanji contained in the dictionary, more did not necessarily mean better. What buyers needed to consider were whether the characters most often in daily use were included and how they were used in the dictionary.

Consumer preference, after all, was responsible in large part for why manufacturers continued to give priority to kanji in word processors. If customers did not want so many characters in the word processor, then there would be cutbacks, but in fact increasing demand, as we have seen, led to the incorporation of not only JIS Level One but also eventually Level Two in the memory banks. Tanaka notes that the title of Natsume Sōseki's famous book *Wagahai wa Neko de aru* (I am a Cat) is sometimes used at the point of sale as a test of the capability of a word processor: intending purchasers type this in hiragana or romaji to see if the correct characters for 'wagahai' (a formal and archaic word for 'I') will come up. Quite a few want to see if the 'wagahai' will come up with the character Sōseki used in 1905 rather than an alternative version, ie to see if older, abstruse characters are included. Tanaka himself reports having boasted to a friend that while the friend's word processor has only one version of 'waga', his own has the proper one, and having taken pleasure in thus asserting superiority on the basis of a character representing something which is very close to being a dead word and which he could hardly even imagine ever using in his own writing. Since the limited memory capacity of the dictionary meant that if one word were included another must be left out, would it not be the worst word processors and not the best, he suggested, which included dead language such as this, particularly the more abstruse of the two character possibilities? And yet many consumers demanded machines with dictionaries which included at least the more common version of this word and preferably also the less common as well (Tanaka 1991: 135–136). The word processor market clearly illustrates the Imade argument outlined by Sugimoto above, that 'Japan's commercial market cannot ignore, and in fact must calculate carefully, spenders' specific predilections'. If consumers wish for 'wagahai', whether from a desire to identify themselves as super-literate persons or merely from a wish to possess a top of the range status symbol, then manufacturers will meet the demand. Japanese buyers in this field cannot be said to be passive consumers of the technology; their active search for its latest refinements impelled the development of better machines throughout the 1980s. The constant upgrading which led in the pre-recession years to instances of functioning word processors being found abandoned in rubbish collection heaps as owners replaced them with the latest model confirms Campbell's comments on the power of 'improvement' in addition to 'erosion' as one of the dynamics explaining the exceptionally high turnover of goods in modern consumerism (Campbell 1992: 54). In Japan, where the disposable culture is well entrenched, as early as 1961 the

White Paper on the economy was subtitled: 'Consumption Is A Virtue – The Era of Throw-away Culture begins' (Yunomae 1996: 102).

Changes in the work force

As with all new technologies which impact on the workplace, the word processor has brought about some changes in the way in which people approach their work. There is of course the obvious change that people no longer have to perform by hand the 'non-human tasks' associated with an information explosion in a country with a script like Japan's, which can now be done by machine. More than this, however, there is an emerging change in the work force since the introduction of word processors and computers, which can be seen in other countries as well: the increased ability to work at home and communicate through fax and modem, particularly (but not solely) for those whose work involves writing, translating or typing services. Much of this has to do with the perceived 'human orientation' of the word processor in an era of 'high information', and it is worth spending some time here to consider this. One of the charges often levelled against personal computers, particularly as game machines, is that they will result in social isolation of human beings from each other as people turn more to machines for entertainment on a one-on-one basis. The image of the computer 'nerd' who relates only to his computer and not to his social peers is well entrenched in popular culture. A 1983 report in Japan on the social impact of electronics picked up on this when it listed as two of the downsides of this technology a growth in control by organisations and the possibility of an increase in the number of social introverts. When people use games, personal computers and word processors, the report noted, they spend a lot of time in dialogue with a machine and less time in contact with human beings; this may promote misanthropy and introversion. A balanced approach to the advance of technology into people's lives is necessary, without engendering pessimism by focusing too much on the perceived disadvantages of distrust of technology, distrust of human beings and introverted behaviour. Choices must be made which will lead to a society where all can live with security and vitality, socially, economically and culturally. There is no doubt that society is changing from a paper society to an electronic one, with people relying on screens, whether television, word processor or computer screens. The spread of the telephone to every house resulted in people writing letters less often. Even photographs, a good example of the paper culture, would become computerised (as they since have). Writing, however, offers a richness of content not found on the screen and retains scope for creativity. A paper culture contains a depth of significance not found in an electronic culture. An over-reliance on on-screen images, the report concluded, might result in the loss of creative ability, the lowering of the quality of culture and damage to the future development of society (Sōgō Kenkyū Kaihatsu Kikō 1983: 10, 111).

In the office, of course, the main change in the nature of the work force was that it became, in theory at least, no longer necessary to maintain specialist typists as in typewriter days, as after a period of training all employees were supposed to be able to produce their own documents on a word processor. In practice, as we know, this has not always been the case, as female employees have been assigned to this task. In addition, the introduction of OA machines such as the word processor was expected to promote a reduction of labour in the support-style office sector, but this was not without its initial problems. The new technology created new work, in that what had formerly been sent out for typing was now done in-house, and the speed of processing information was slower than it had been before because of the unfamiliarity of the medium. As these problems were solved, forecast the 1983 report, there would appear a labour force surplus to requirements, with the attendant problem of how to redistribute these people. Given that many new support-style offices were appearing with systems using computers, it would be possible to absorb them, but a massive program of education would be required. The many women working in the software industry, which allowed flexibility for part-time or at-home work, could work from terminals at home, as had the specialist Japanese typists before the advent of the word processor who had used company typewriters at home (Sōgō Kenkyū Kaihatsu Kikō 1983: 67, 71).

'In practice', Morris-Suzuki noted in 1988, 'the technological changes occurring in Japan are altering both the content of work and the structure of employment, and these two facets of change are closely intertwined with each other' (Morris-Suzuki 1988: 107). We have already seen how the content of work has changed, with a variety of once separate tasks such as document production and filing now combined in a single machine. Morris-Suzuki looks in detail at the effect of office automation on the role of female workers, who within a relatively short space of time compared to western countries have found their job descriptions metamorphosing from that of general office worker to specialist keyboard operator. She cites a 1983 survey of office automation in NEC's Tamagawa plant, which found (and I quote in full) that:

- all women workers, without distinction between general office workers and typists, became keyboard operators
- the number of women who spent all day operating word processors and terminals increased
- as a result, general office workers began to perform work which gave rise to occupational health problems
- the number of people complaining of poor health because of chronic shoulder pains, tired eyes, nervous stress and ill health caused by air-conditioning systems increased
- in the case of women workers, when appointed to work on word processors and terminals, they were simply given the operating manual and did not receive any training. This policy of letting them learn as they performed their work was described as 'on-the-job training'.

What actually happened as a result of office automation was not a freeing up of time for less mundane tasks for the general office worker as had been predicted for the information society but rather an increase in the productivity of clerical work which benefited the upper echelons of managers and technicians whose work was supported by the office staff (Morris-Suzuki 1988: 121–122). In addition to this change, there has also been an expansion of the mostly female part-time, temporary and contract employment sector of the workforce due to office automation, a situation welcomed by employers because the rapidly changing nature of the technology optimally requires a flexible workforce which will not need the retraining in new skills required in the case of permanent employees. 'Technological change ... tends to reduce the useful lifespan of work-related knowledge to a length shorter than the normal working life of human beings' (144). This has led to the rise in Japan of the *haken* system of contract workers, who include women in their twenties and thirties who, often in the absence of any other suitable employment, work for secretarial agencies and are contracted out to perform such tasks on a temporary basis as word-processing and general office work. Many such women have obtained their skills at their own expense by participating in training courses at private agencies. The sense of isolation among these workers which constant moving entails is one of the less desirable social consequences of office automation (Morris-Suzuki 1988: 146,148)

By 1993, the number of contract employment agencies in Japan had grown to around 8,600, with 440,000 registered workers, with the industry recording steady growth following a temporary slump after the economic downturn began in 1990. The changes wrought by the recession in the personnel practices of large companies, which had formerly focussed on the lifetime employment system and a seniority-based promotion system, have increased demand for contract employees, many of whom now include middle-aged men laid off by their employers. Furthermore, the rapid pace of technological development has seen contract agencies take on an important educational function, instructing job-seekers in personal computer operation and other skills before sending them to companies seeking people with such training. The Ministry of Labour is planning to add twelve new categories to the sixteen currently permitted to contract employees; one of the new ones will be office automation instruction, so that contract employees with the skills required will take on a training role in the companies to which they are sent (Nanbu 1996: 16–17).

To a certain extent, the charge of isolating people from human contact through interaction with a machine could be made against the word processor, particularly as people are now able to work more at home and send work in without actual human contact. Newspaper 'letters to the editor' pages during the 1980s reflected this concern that new media would damage human social discourse. A point in the word processor's favour, however, is that it uses a natural language rather than a computer language and may thus be considered 'human-oriented' compared to, say, a computer game. In fact, given the intellectual tasks this machine is able to perform through its various functions, it could be considered an exemplar of a desirable machine-user interface (Hamaguchi 1986: 196). This view of the user-friendliness of the word processor is seconded by a writer who describes using one as like having a conversation with another person. The machine is a writing implement, true, but rather than holding it in the hand like a pen, one sits down to face it. Unlike a typewriter, it has some particular functions of its own. When he gets up in the middle of something and goes away somewhere, he feels when he comes back as though the cursor has been sitting in the same place waiting patiently for his return (Suzuki 1988: 20). It is doubtful, however, whether this romanticised view of the personal nature of interaction with a word processor would occur to many users. Regardless of this 'chat with a machine' aspect, it is undeniably the case that working at home produces physical isolation from one's colleagues, despite the availability of modems, faxes and phones.

This trade-off between convenience and social interaction has become, in Japan as in the west, one of the biggest social challenges of the information age, signalling a significant shift in the spatial and communicative foundations of interpersonal interaction. If people work at home, suggests the 1990 *White Paper on Living Conditions,* that will lead to a savings in company expenses and an extension of the potential labour force, but other things will become more difficult, eg evaluations of individual performance, management of working hours and allocation of diversified roles in tasks. On the personal side, although it will allow more work opportunities for older people and for women, allowing them to work at their own pace with more free time and without commuting problems, it will also become more difficult to demarcate the boundary between work and private life, and will weaken collegiality among employees as the individual will no longer have to fit into the company or even attend the company daily to do specific tasks. If the trend continues, the report concludes, it will become even more important for manufacturers and developers to pay attention to making the user-machine interface easy to negotiate for all segments of society (Keizai Kikakuchō 1990: 186, 192).

There is certainly no shortage of interest in working at home since the advent of the word processor and other forms of new media. Morris-Suzuki cites an instance of a secretarial agency that advertised 60 jobs for home-based word processor operators and received 4,500 applications, most from married women with children. Despite the perceived attractions of home-based computer outwork of this nature, however, it also gives rise to problems such as stress caused by attempting to get on with the work while caring for children and difficulty in monitoring health hazards attendant on prolonged word processor use. The work is controlled in a variety of ways by the company, which can set the loaned word processing equipment to predetermined formats which will monitor the number of keystrokes and the time taken to complete the task. Through work at home, the employer is able to shed much of the cost of employee training, office space and electricity bills, leading Morris-Suzuki to conclude that 'the indirect exploitation of women's unpaid labour in the household is likely to be replaced by the direct exploitation of women's paid labour through home-based work' (Morris-Suzuki 1988: 172–174). The relationship between the public and the private in home-based work thus becomes blurred, with the family domain becoming to a certain extent embedded in the wider domain of work.

Within Japan itself, then, word processing technology has had a significant impact on conventions relating to the role of writing in general and in interpersonal communication in particular, on the lifestyles of its users, on the workforce, and on consumer identity construction. The following chapter will look at how the technology has affected Japan in an international context.

CHAPTER FIVE

Implications for International Communication

We have seen in the foregoing chapters that word processing technology has played a significant role in both the construction of the information era and its associated affective concerns within Japan itself. What have been the consequences for Japan's interface with the rest of the world? Despite the push for Japanese to become an international language like English or French, the writing system is often seen as a barrier to achieving this goal. While word processing technology has enabled Japanese-language computing, there has still been difficulty with international standards of various kinds and a relatively late takeup of the Internet. What implications does the electronic handling of characters have for the transmission of data between countries and for Japan's international presence on the Internet? Is it true, as has been argued by advocates of romanisation, that the continued use of characters in the computer age, and in particular on the Net, acts to reinforce a barrier between Japan and the rest of the world? This chapter will examine first some of the views on practical difficulties with international standards and then the argument that the continued use of characters on the Internet constitutes a kind of language nationalism.

We might best begin by briefly examining the growth of the Internet in Japan and the spread of the Japanese language online. Internet use, although slow to start, has surged ahead in Japan in recent years, although Japan still lags behind many other advanced countries. In Australia in August 1998, for example, 23.4% of the total population was on-line; the figure for Japan in October was only 11.1% (NUA Internet Surveys 1998). The strength of the yen may have been a factor behind slower Web use rates in Japan: until recently, the strong yen meant that even expensive American developers were cheaper to use than Japanese companies (Japan MarkeTracker 18/8/1998). The 80% growth in the number of Japanese Web pages reported by the Ministry of Posts and Telecommunication (MPT) in 1998 may have been due to the weaker yen allowing small Japanese companies to become competitive in providing such services. The high cost of phone calls in Japan is also a factor: a January 1999 Nikkei Market Access survey shows that peak Internet use starts promptly at 11pm, when discounted phone rates begin, and peaks again at 7–8am (Japan MarkeTracker 2/3/1999).

Despite a relatively slow start, however, Japanese Internet usage has burgeoned. Between June and September 1996, the growth in Japanese listings on the Web was triple that of English, with consumers as well as companies contributing to this (NUA Internet Surveys, 7/9/1996). In September 1997, Japan had the highest growth rate in Internet Service Providers in Asia, at 200%, and annual growth rates for 1996 to 2001 were predicted to average at 28.3% (NUA Internet Surveys 18/9/1997). Research carried out in June 1997 indicated that the number of Internet users in 1996 had nearly doubled from the previous year (Global Strategies 1998). The explosive growth of the World Wide Web appeared from 1998 figures to have settled down a little, but use of the Internet and e-mail alone has been rising (Japan Biztech 1998). With the successful development of various kinds of Japanese e-mail software, e-mail use appears to be driving Internet growth: a Nikkei Market Access survey reported in a quarterly survey analysis that 9.3 million people used e-mail, up 27% from the previous survey, compared with only a 14% increase in the number of web users (Japan MarkeTracker 20/10/1998).

Internet chat services are popular with Japanese users, and completely Japanese versions are now available (such as, eg, the Japanese version of iChat found since mid-1998 at 'P's pub', a chat room on the online service of ISP GrR HomeNet (http: //www.plala.or.jp/). A Nikkei Market Access survey conducted between September and December 1998 to determine where Japanese web surfers spent most time found that chat sites, at 24% of the time respondents spent on line, were the biggest draw, ahead of 17.9% for search engine sites (Japan MarkeTracker 26/1/1999).

A demographic survey of Internet users in Japan carried out in September 1998 found that 56% came from the Kantō area around Tokyo (compared to only 18% from the Kansai area around Osaka, Japan's second biggest city); 60% were fully employed; students had slipped from 15% to 12% of the Internet population; and 90% of women online were between 20 and 39, compared to 75% of men (Fujitsu Research Institute 1998). Another survey conducted November–December 1998 by Nikkei Multimedia found that women accounted for only 17.2% of Japanese Internet users, but that women made up 38.8% of new Internet users (a steep rise compared to 8.2% of new users before March 1993) (Nikkei Multimedia 1998). Other surveys conducted by Fujitsu Research Institute (November 1998) and the Internet Association of Japan (June 1998) confirm this move on to the Internet by Japanese women; the latter suggested that as many as 25% (more than the 17.2% 9/1998 Fujitsu survey) of Japanese using the Net are women. Whatever the total figure may be, it seems clear from all reported data that an increasing number of new users (less than six months on the Web) are women, with most of them logging on for entertainment rather than work-related reasons (Japan MarkeTracker 22/12/1998).

The Internet in Japan, then, though it has penetrated to date less than in the US and other countries such as Australia, is flourishing. The Japanese language now functions globally in the electronic community, and the invention of word processing technology has been a major contributing factor to this. While English retains its pre-eminence as the international language of cyberspace, there is plenty of evidence from Internet surveys conducted by bodies such as research agency eMarketer that on-line users of other languages are catching up fast. Non-English speakers today constitute the fastest-growing group of new Internet users, particularly those using Spanish, German, Portuguese, Chinese, Japanese and the Scandinavian languages (eMarketer, 30/6/1998). A March 1999 survey by Global Reach reported that non-English speaking users now account for nearly 50%, up from less than 10% four years ago. While about 100 million of the 180 million subscribers speak English, there are now 14.2 million users each of Spanish and Japanese (eMarketer 17/3/99).

As we saw in Chapter One, Japanese had already become the second most widely used language other than English on the Internet by August 1998 (Global Internet Statistics 1998), a month after a survey reported that JP top level domain names ranked fifth in the number of hosts supported on the Internet (Network Wizards, 7/ 1998) following the liberalisation of Internet service providers in Japan two years earlier. By September 1998, reported the Ministry of Posts and Telecommunication, there were more than 18 million web pages in Japan, up from 10 million only seven months earlier. Working from the assumption that each page contains 2,000 characters, the MPT calculated, that equated to a total of 36 billion characters, exceeding the total number of characters published in Japanese newspapers and magazines in a year (Japan MarkeTracker 1/12/1998). The Japanese-language presence on the Internet is now therefore incontrovertibly well established.

Since the advent of computers, the old argument that characters hamper meaningful exchange of ideas has been extended to include electronic media: in order to overcome the difficulty caused by the extra work involved in processing them by comparison with the alphabet, Japan should adopt romanisation (eg Unger 1987, Yamada 1989, Hannas 1997). The romanisation debate is in my view really a dead issue since the invention of character-capable word processing technology. The view of the Japanese script as a barrier, however, still lingers, as we shall see. One who firmly believes that the perpetuation of kanji is handicapping Japan's progress on the international scene is Yamada Hisao, who argues that characters are a major obstacle to the transmission of information between countries. In 1989, Yamada wrote of a plan to exchange resources relating to scientific results between several European countries and Japan, which was to be funded by the governments involved. Despite Japanese representations, a decision was taken that only the western alphabet would be used in the project. As a result, all Japanese research results would have to be romanised; only Japan would have to bear this extra burden. This was quite a separate issue, Yamada commented, from that of whether or not anyone else could read Japanese: it was about the problem of using characters for information exchange and communication. Even if one took the line that if non-Japanese wanted to read Japanese materials they could learn the language, the fact is that data in Japanese could not be sent. This would cause major problems for international economic competition and for transmission of culture outside Japan.

Yamada's own view is that characters ought to give way to romanisation in the computer age. The appearance of the word processor has indubitably enabled Japanese to take a renewed interest in their culture. For him, however, characters are not an inextricable component of Japanese culture. Whenever there is a move to change something old (as in this case, with the suggestion that romanisation should replace characters), the issue of the transmission of the cultural heritage is always raised. Many believe that if the Japanese people cannot read characters they will forget their cultural heritage. In Europe, however, there are very few who can read their national literary treasures in the language in which they were written; most rely on translations, which meet their needs just as well. It is entirely possible, Yamada argues, to replace characters in the same way while still retaining a particular cultural ethos; a strong culture has nothing to fear from this (Yamada 1989: 1208–1209). In other words, the true nature of culture is not dependent on the medium (in this case characters) of its expression. As an advocate of romanisation, Yamada rejects the idea that if people cannot read characters their language abilities will somehow be weakened as a result: surely the strength of the national language depends not on the script but on the extent to which the entire populace can read and write expressively. That ability has increased greatly compared with the past, thanks to the script reforms of the twentieth century, and in his view simplifying the script further by getting rid of characters would only continue that trend.

Yamada cited the then comparatively low rate of Internet usage in Japan as further evidence of the malign influence of characters. The use of e-mail and remote databases, spreading rapidly in other developed countries, lagged behind in Japan. While there might be many reasons for this, some specialists had imputed it to the fact that keyboard input is a nuisance because of the complexity of the Japanese writing system. The number of LAN (Local Area Networks) connected to the Internet in the United States was 5,571 in June 1993, whereas in Japan it was only 257. This clearly showed that Japanese intellectuals were still isolated from the rest of the world, in large part due to kanji (Yamada 1994: 47–48).

Between 1997 and 1998, the number of Internet hosts in Japan increased to 496,427, a 585% increase on the 1994 figure. This still indicated lower Internet usage than in the United States and Australia (Australia, for instance, had 397,460 hosts for a population of 18 million, whereas Japan's hosts, though on paper larger, serviced a population of 125 million). Was this lower rate due to language, ie to characters, or to other structural factors? As early as 1986, Kumon Shunpei of GLOCOM worried that the explanation did indeed lie in language. The linguistic domination of English on e-mail networks, for example, even on some within Japan, meant that Japanese users would 'lurk', accessing information but contributing none because of fear of exposing their poor English skills and because Japan's 'traditional culture' did not predispose them towards electronic conferencing as a forum for the general exchange of information and opinions. Even if people wanted to communicate in Japanese, he commented, few computer software packages at that time allowed effective handling of kanji. If input were restricted to kana or romaji the result was hard for Japanese to read, so the easiest thing was just to lurk and read other people's messages, a trend which was resulting in only non-Japanese transmitting to the networks (Kumon 1986: 68–69). It is possible that the popularity of stand-alone word processors in the 1980s may have contributed to the paucity of Japanese-language word processing packages for computers, and hence to Internet participation, during this period, although of course that is not the only reason for the slower rate of computer use in Japan. Since then, however, the number of Japanese-language Web pages and discussion groups which can be accessed internationally has steadily increased, and discussion lists for those who are interested in Japan and Japanese regularly feature hints and questions on where to find the software for handling Japanese script. Japanese-language pages can now easily be read from computers whose software is English-dependent by using packages such as Asiaview and Kanjikit, to name just two, and of course standard commercial packages such as the Japanese version of Word have been available since the early 1990s. Many important Web sites in Japan have both English and Japanese versions, others just Japanese. The click of a button to indicate choice of language on multi-language versions enables Japanese to claim back the territory, as it were, from English in a way which print media do not readily allow.

Another area which in Yamada's experience exposes the kanji problem to the eyes of the world is that of international standards. The ISO (International Standards Organisation) is charged with deciding various standards or norms on a worldwide scale. Kanji have proved a sticking point in several areas where standardisation has been sought, such as electronic communications, office machines and so forth, and there have been quite a few occasions when it has been difficult to come to terms with the alphabet countries on certain points. Because of this, many international conferences have been held; sending specialist members to these has been a big burden in terms of time to the specialist delegates and a financial burden for the industrial groups involved. Even the ISO 10646 kanji code set (Unicode) arrived at after long hard work by the ISO's SC2 subcommittee did not fully meet the needs of all of the CJK kanji countries (China, Japan, Korea) because it was mainly decided at the disposition of the leading western countries[1]. Even so, Japan decided to accept it as an important international standard, despite whispers in other ISO subcommittees that it might be ignored, at least in the short term, because of its complexity and the likely impact that this might have on quite a few other international standards of the ISO, such as those for computer programming language and electronic communication protocols (Yamada 1994: 48). Sakamura Ken, of Tokyo University's TRON[2] project, agrees with Yamada's reservations about Unicode, commenting that its biggest problem is that of unification: characters with similar shapes are lumped together despite the fact that they come from three different countries, each of which only uses its own version of the characters, in order to save the expense of creating separate codes for each country. In Sakamura's view, the code was developed by people from non-kanji countries (the United States had been instrumental in pushing for it) without any real understanding of the compatibility needs of the separate countries, purely for marketing reasons (Sakamura 1998: 3).

A 1996 article on kanji and the Internet confirmed Yamada's concern with the usefulness of the ISO 10646 (Unicode) in meeting the needs of each of the kanji countries and promoting the exchange of kanji information between them. In it, Murata Tadayoshi of Yokohama University questioned the need to keep on increasing the kanji code lists when there remained areas of non-reciprocity between China and Japan in code lists which he considered inappropriate to the Internet age where kanji are transcending borders on to the international scene. The JIS supplementary kanji code was added to Levels One and Two in Japan in 1990 because of perceptions that the existing levels were not sufficient, but no Japanese word processors or personal computers incorporated the extra characters. The UNICODE, adopted by Japan in 1995, contains 20,902 characters. Even that is not considered sufficient: the TRON project is working on codifying around 50,000 characters.

Murata himself questioned this quantitative approach to the matter, noting that if the object of these codes were to cover all the characters to be found in dictionaries then even 50,000 would not suffice, as a Chinese dictionary which contains 55,000 characters had already been published. Rather than concentrating on codifying the many fossilised characters this number involves, a more pressing need is to address the remaining needs of international information exchange using kanji. The JIS codes and China's GB Codes, drawn up in the early days of computer handling of kanji, took into account only each country's own characters. This led to some problems when reporting international news: certain Chinese characters which are not in JIS have been appearing frequently in Japanese newspapers and magazines, whereas in China the fact that the GB codes do not contain six characters created in Japan and used very commonly in place and personal names makes it difficult to write these names on a Chinese word processor. The GB code Level One contains 3,755 characters which are considered sufficient to meet the requirements of everyday Chinese writing. The same consideration operates in the JIS Level One in Japan, where the number of characters is smaller but is supplemented by the different readings which are assigned to each and by the use of kana. Unfortunately, however, neither the Chinese nor the Japanese Level One contains sufficient characters to cover the other country's first level, but Murata's research found that around 90% of Chinese-language information could be covered by adding a further sixteen characters to the JIS Level One. In the Internet era, when Japanese and Chinese homepages are proliferating and the major newspapers can be read on the Net, it is important, he argued, to aid the transmission of kanji-based information by constructing a kanji code system which covers all the general-use characters for each kanji country (Murata 1996: 90–91).

These views on the matter highlight the ongoing debate surrounding standards for encoding characters. The first version of Unicode attracted widespread criticism because it lacked certain characters; it had been developed without much in the way of liaison with East Asian countries. Following consultation with those regions affected, a second version proved more effective and was backed by MITI. There is still, however, a body of opinion holding out for independent Japanese-specific codes rather than a multi-country approach.

A further interesting if depressing aspect of international information exchange which Yamada discovered from surveys carried out by the National Center for Science Information Systems was that even Japanese scientific journals published in English were not often read overseas. The Japan Information Processing Society, for example, one of the biggest academic societies in Japan, put out an English-language journal with articles carefully vetted for quality, but only about one hundred copies a year were sold through overseas subscription. This situation remained unchanged over a ten-year period, despite the good international reputation of Japanese computer technology, perhaps because although the text of the articles was in English, the bibliographic citations in many cases listed only Japanese sources (ie written in Japanese). In the west the list of references is considered an important part of the article, and western scientists usually read the article while referring to the list as necessary (Yamada 1991: 285).

Of the overall impact of word processing technology, which has made possible the perpetuation of characters, Yamada's assessment is not favourable. Certainly it has vastly improved the handling of documents in Japan, but the improvement is really only a matter of comparison between the Japan of before and the Japan of today; the efficiency of document production in western countries remains far superior. As can be seen by the flourishing of e-mail in western countries compared to Japan, the west has recently increased the gap even further. Yamada's attendance at ISO conferences has reinforced his understanding of just how great a burden characters impose on Japanese social activities. Where the input speed of characters is slow, the speed of transmission of information falls as a result. Although Japan has one of the highest GNPs in the world, this does not translate into a sense of comfort or ease in society at large, and Yamada somewhat ambitiously attributes this in large measure to the complexity of handling documents imposed by characters. The cost of factory production has come down rapidly because of the widespread use of automation technology; the future of office productivity, however, remains unclear. In Yamada's view, the fact that Japanese people have become accustomed to inefficient document handling has desensitised them to the fact of inefficiency in offices and the inefficiency of activities in general in Japan (1991: 287–288).

A recent book by Hannas argued that computers, far from allowing equal facility of handling to the two script types (alphabet and characters), are in fact accentuating the gap, and that the greater the number of computer applications that are developed, the more noticeable will be the performance differences. 'The lack of conventions for word division and the absence of universal standards for managing character scripts in general have had a devastating impact on computerised language processing in East Asia' (Hannas 1997: 262). Hannas agrees with Yamada that 'the absence of shared standards on how to manage East Asian writing systems has affected the development of the East Asian computer industry as a whole' (263). In his view, the fact that character scripts require a second level of conversion vis-à-vis the alphabet will be sufficient in the long run to effect language policy changes leading to the replacement of characters. Maybe he would be right were it not for the weight of tradition and affective attachment to characters of their users, which in my view will outweigh (at least for the foreseeable future) the practical advantages which romanisation would undoubtedly confer.

This brings us to the issue of whether or not the continued use of kanji on the Internet which this technology makes possible is really an example of language nationalism or not. On the global scene, the technology may be viewed from one angle as having enabled Japan to 'maintain its difference' in an era of increasing globalisation of communications and heterogenisation, in many areas, of cultural practices. The belief that first office automation and later computer-based communication would require romanisation as an absolute basis (irrespective of other considerations of relative efficiencies) has without doubt been laid to rest by the character-capable word processor. But is the use of Japanese on the Net really an example of language nationalism, or is it simply a matter of technology supporting infrastructure? In order to answer this question, we must first examine the argument that the Japanese language, and by extension the script, functions as an effective barrier between Japan and other countries.

Both Western and Japanese scholars have from time to time argued (eg Miller 1982, Befu 1983, Dale 1986) that the way in which Japanese view their language contributes to a kind of language nationalism which functions to emphasise the separateness of the Japanese people from others in the affective as well as linguistic sense. This is not the way in which the term 'language nationalism' is normally employed: 'language nationalism' (or 'linguistic nationalism') is more commonly taken to refer to the central role that language has often played in modern nationalist movements, as for example in Israel and Ireland. It is true that the establishment of a standard version of the national language and the modernisation of written Japanese played an important part in the overall modernisation of Japan, and that rhetoric with strong nationalistic overtones was often employed in that debate (see Twine 1991). Given the unimodal linguistic situation in Japan, however, the question of what the national language itself should be was never in doubt. The manner in which the term 'language nationalism' has been used to refer to Japan has centred instead on the manner in which the language (and in particular the script) is perceived as forming a cherished linguistic barrier between Japan and the rest of the world, moating the intellectual life of the home country in a way which, until recently, comparatively few could breach from outside.

Essentialism and internationalisation

The publishing genre known as Nihonjinron, or discourses on what it means to be Japanese, has been one of the conspicuous features of Japanese intellectual production of the last thirty years or so. Such discourses invariably stress the uniqueness of the Japanese people and their cultural arrangements as measured against the western Other, the special and separate nature of their social discourse, and even, in an extreme manifestation, the special modification of the physical structure of the Japanese brain (Tsunoda 1985). The Nihonjinron genre has a significant following both in Japan and overseas and has been used as a powerful tool in reinforcing a separatist ideology. It functions as a wall of words emphasising Japanese exceptionalism, with the aim of setting the Japanese people as a monolithic and to a large extent unknowable whole off from the rest of the world. Many writers (notably Dale1986; Mouer and Sugimoto 1989; and Yoshino 1992) have analysed the significance of this belief in a substantial corpus of work challenging the stereotyped views of Japan. Their work, joined in the field of language research by Maher and Yashiro (1995) and Maher and Macdonald (1995), has done much to expose the diversity beneath the surface of this purportedly seamless whole and point up aspects of social heterogeneity which Japan shares with many other parts of the world.

The conviction that Japan is unique has been described as a kind of compensatory technique deriving from Japan's centuries-long history of situating itself psychologically on the cultural periphery of great powers, initially China, later Europe, then America (Wilkinson 1991). The myth of primordial national identity is a self-consciously created reaction to the process of absorbing foreign influence (Buell 1994). The undoubted westernisation of Japan during its modern period, far from weakening the notion of Japanese uniqueness, has been seen as a defensive strategy which shores up the inner core. It is a strategy which exemplifies what Clifford (1988) describes as 'the need to stage authenticity in opposition to external, often dominating alternatives' (12), what Mouer and Sugimoto (1983) have called 'a mystique ... in which Japan is hidden in mist' (277).

Against this construction of an essentialist Japanese national identity we must balance the fact that, far from remaining aloof, Japan has since the 1980s been following a path of *kokusaika* (internationalisation) intended to result in a more open and cosmopolitan society. Globalisation, a related phenomenon which shares similarities with the way internationalisation is understood in Japan, has been so widely discussed over the last fifteen years that Waters (1995) refers to the term as the defining concept of the 1990s. He himself defines globalisation as 'a social process in which the constraints of geography on social and cultural arrangements recede and in which people become increasingly aware that they are receding' (3). In a globalised world, social and cultural life might no longer be determined by territoriality and geographical location might cease to be a predictor of social practice and preference – in other words, there would be a disjuncture between culture and locale. In many areas it is clear that this is happening already. Examples abound of the diverse manifestations of cultural heterogeneity in everyday life practices across the globe, and Japan itself is a good illustration of this. In terms of culture, what is presented as local is many cases recognised to be in fact the result of earlier global interactions. In the case of Japan, the local 'pure' Japanese culture so often fixed in binary opposition to westernisation in the Nihonjinron literature is in fact the result of centuries of interaction with China and earlier encounters with the west.

The Nihonjinron genre rejects this flaccidity of boundaries and engages in a determined reconsolidation of borders. Meanwhile, however, the government's policy of 'internationalisation' has included linguistic and cultural initiatives which contribute to the increasing porosity of those borders. There has been much debate as to just what internationalisation means in relation to Japanese society (as opposed to, say, economic markets where its meaning is fairly clear). One of the issues debated has been whether internationalisation necessarily means a diminution of 'Japaneseness', ie is it just another synonym for westernisation, or whether it offers the real chance of a two-way exchange of ideas with the only loss that of insularity.

Passin (1983) outlines a dual scenario: the belief that Japanese were so different from everybody else meant either that Japanese culture would hinder necessary internationalisation or that the independent contribution of the Japanese to international society would come precisely by holding on to unique qualities and cultural traditions. Leading globalisation theorist Roland Robertson (1992) supports the second of these alternatives, arguing that the manner in which a nation interacts on the global scene will continue to be mediated by 'internal' features of its society. Robertson's comment is embedded within a discussion of globality and Japanese religion, but we may also usefully extend this to language and script. The problem of language is central to the internationalisation debate in Japan. The writing system is, as we shall see, an outstanding example of a nation's global interaction being mediated by an internal feature of its society.

Language nationalism

The supposed unique impenetrability of the Japanese language has long been advanced as one of the factors involved in demarcating the barriers between Japan and the rest of the world. Miller's 1982 book *Japan's Modern Myth* demonstrates (while at the same time debunking) the manner in which this myth constructs an indissoluble link between the country's language and race, culture and even morality, and functions as a linguistic rampart. 'It is the myth that argues that there is a need for foreigners to learn the Japanese language but also simultaneously claims that the Japanese language is so uniquely difficult that it is all but impossible for anyone to learn it, whether Japanese or foreigner' (20). Dale (1986) likewise takes issue with the manner in which, in the Nihonjinron tradition, perfectly ordinary Japanese words have been loaded with ideologically constructed 'nuances' which can ostensibly be understood only by Japanese, so that attempts by foreigners to translate are doomed to failure. What is happening here, he warns, is 'an academic metadiscourse, implicated with intertextual reverberations of uniqueness, that raises a semantic bamboo curtain between Japan and the outside world' (61). To understand this is to begin to see the structures of mystification which underlie the construction of essentialist cultural discourse in Japan, what Miller characterises as a kind of self-Orientalisation.

Outside academic circles, the view in the world at large of the language as a barrier remains as robust as when in 1918, in a book ironically dedicated to debunking the myth of Asiatic mystery, Clarke wrote of the Japanese commercial man that 'his language is extremely difficult; it is a formidable barrier to complete interchange of thought with the foreigner ... this language barrier, believe me, accounts for nine-tenths of the "Asiatic mystery"' (3–4). Over fifty years later, this view was still current in popular writing about Japan. Bernard Rudofsky's *The Kimono Mind* (1974), for example, representative of the many lightweight guides to Japan and its people which purport to interpret Japan to the rest of the world, said of the language that it 'looms as a never-never land which few dare to explore ... anybody who has acquired by some gruesome brain manipulation the faculty to speak Japanese realises how futile were his efforts. His difficulty in communicating with the Japanese has merely grown in depth' (156–157). Later still, we find scholar and diplomat Endymion Wilkinson (1991) still speaking of language difficulties as one of the major sources of misunderstanding between the Japanese and other peoples, and citing the well-known Japanese perception that their language is 'uniquely difficult for foreigners to learn'.

This view does not sit well with the scale of the language promotion activities undertaken by the Foreign Ministry (within which the Japan Foundation is located), which are evidence that Japan has poured large amounts of money into an attempt to make its language accessible to foreigners. As a result of Japan's economic status there has been a marked increase in the number of foreign learners of Japanese, which the current economic woes have done little to stem. The 1995 report issued by the Foundation on the number of learners around the world gives a figure of 1,623,455, a huge leap compared to the 1979 total of 127,167 (Japan Foundation 1995). The Japan Foundation has not been alone in promoting the study of Japanese: in Australia, for example, the federal and various state governments have instituted large-scale programs for the teaching of Asian languages, prominent among them Japanese. Both the economic importance of Japan and the consequent language teaching programs have contributed to the internationalisation of Japan in the sense of having provided motivation and opportunity for non-Japanese to learn the language and thereby interact at grass-roots level with Japanese people. Other moves in the direction of a more cosmopolitan society have been the expansion of the number of foreign students studying in Japan and the Education Ministry's JET program (Japan Exchange and Teaching Program, inaugurated in 1987) aimed at facilitating the learning of English by employing native English speakers as assistant teachers in Japanese junior and senior high schools.

The belief among Japanese at large that foreigners cannot learn the Japanese language, however, remains strong. In the early 1990s, there was a controversial attempt within the National Language Research Institute in Tokyo to develop a program of 'simplified Japanese' (*Kan'yaku Nihongo*) for foreigners, to make the task of learning the language easier by paring down some of the linguistic complexities to a minimum, resulting in a kind of pidgin Japanese. This program attracted strong criticism from both Japanese and non-Japanese alike, and it is interesting that it was developed almost in competition, as it were, with the Foreign Ministry's program of teaching 'real Japanese' overseas. Befu (1983) draws out the implications of the widespread belief in the unique difficulty of Japanese, emphasising the role played by the language as a barrier between Japan and the rest of the world and concluding that 'the question of sociolinguistic integrity is inextricably tied in with the Japanese belief that Japanese language, culture and race are one' (250). Discussing the genetic theory of language transmission in Japan, he argues that such a theory arms the Japanese with 'a secure line of defence in maintaining their separateness and distinctness even in the face of an onslaught of foreign cultural diffusion'(258).

Have things changed since 1983, given the continuing spread of Japanese language education outside Japan (and of course, within Japan itself?) A recent program broadcast on Monitor Radio by journalist Andrew Horvat, long-term resident of Japan, would suggest that such experiences, though by no means universal, are still common. Yoshino's 1992 study of the reception of Nihonjinron theories among

Japanese educators and businessmen also cites similar instances. Befu himself argues in the Monitor program, however, that 'language nationalism' is now on the wane as more and more Japanese travel abroad and acquire foreign friends; in a 1989 survey, he found that more respondents (43%) disagreed than agreed (36%) with the proposition that foreigners could not completely master the language (Manabe, Befu et al. 1989).

The script factor

How does the script fit into the language nationalism view? The Japanese writing system is viewed by both Japanese and foreigners alike as an important element in the 'linguistic barrier' between Japan and the rest of the world. Over the years it has been discussed as a significant factor in discouraging foreigners from learning the language, assuming that they want to read it as well as speak it. It has also been seen both inside and outside Japan as a problem for the Japanese themselves; the arguments advanced to support this view have been broadly based on the grounds of educational efficiency, literacy, office automation and international interaction (see Gottlieb 1995).

It is certainly true that the writing system, and in particular kanji, has always been both a privileged signifier of Japanese culture and an ideologically productive site of discourse within that culture. The concept of the inalienable right of characters to represent the Japanese spirit is of course ironic in view of the fact that characters did not originate in Japan at all but were adopted from China. After their adoption, however, characters were transformed into something in Japan which through its agency helped reduce Japan's position as barbarian periphery to China – a writing system where none had been before, the means whereby the literature, history and religious thought of a people could be preserved and developed and claims could be made to being a civilisation. To a large extent it is recognition of this symbolic significance which has perpetuated the use of characters in the face of instrumental arguments against them. Since 1945, the script has been rationalised from its previous complexity to a more conveniently manageable state (see Gottlieb 1995). Characters retain a solid and unyielding following, to the point where many Japanese identify the language itself with kanji and by extension – if ethnicity is identified by the language – with their very identity as Japanese (Brown 1986).

Outside Japan, the script is probably the single most effective factor in convincing the rest of the world that Japanese is 'a difficult language'. As Miller (1969: vii) pointed out, the Japanese language, like Chinese, has long been hidden behind its orthography, overlooked in favour of the script. Western attitudes to the script have been by and large products of Orientalist exoticism. We find abundant examples in the literature on Japan of an at times almost rhapsodical glorification of the beauty and mystery of characters (see, for example, Lafcadio Hearn's 1894 writings in King 1984: 21), in which the orthography is made to reinforce Japan's otherness in western eyes. It is this enduring vision of exoticism, coupled with fear of the magnitude of the task of learning characters, which has led to the script being perceived as a barrier between Japan and the western world.

In Japan's relations with the outside world, then, the script often presents a major psychological barrier in the eyes of non-Japanese-speakers, not those motivated to undertake serious study of the language but rather the majority who view the language through the veil of the script without any real knowledge of how it functions. This is of course another reason why the arguments for romanisation we saw in Chapter One have been advanced ever since Japan's modern contact with the west. With the late nineteenth century push towards westernisation which followed the Meiji Restoration, claims were advanced at first by individual scholars and later by small interest groups on behalf of romanisation (see Twine 1991). Underpinning these calls was a vision of relative modernity, that perception of a gap between Japan and the modern which provided the motivation for many of the changes instituted after the Meiji Period. These supporters met with no success. The first half of the twentieth century saw the formation of other romanisation groups (see Gottlieb 1995), polarised as to spelling but pushing among other things the line we have already seen, that romanisation would close the technology gap with the west, facilitate international communication and assist office automation. Apart from a brief flurry of interest during the Occupation and on the part of some members of the immediate postwar National Language Council, there has never been any real prospect that these ideas would be taken seriously, and today the Japan Romanisation Society has only around 350 members.

Today, when the exotic is no longer far away or largely unknowable, technology is often seen as functioning to break down national barriers, to replace formerly fairly discrete cultural discourses with lines of global discourse not dependent on locality. In many instances, particularly those related to the media, this is indubitably so. The invention of Japanese word processing technology, however, might perhaps be interpreted as an instance of technology functioning not to break down this particular 'barrier' but rather to perpetuate it - if barrier it is - by knocking the stuffing out of the argument for romanisation. It is never only questions of economic progress which inform technology development; there are issues of cultural change to be considered as well. The benefits of romanisation to Japan have of course always been advanced in terms of pragmatic considerations such as educational and corporate efficiency, but the argument has never been considered sufficiently persuasive in cultural terms. Romanisation advocates have been considered a kind of 'ratbag fringe'. The economic benefits they presented as contingent on improved office efficiency have been decisively outweighed by cultural considerations successfully linked with the development of new technologies, specifically the fax and later the word processor, not to mention the incontrovertible evidence of

Japan's economic progress despite the use of characters. And as we saw in Chapter One, the matter of the local infrastructure weighs heavily against change.

Kanji on the Internet

James Clifford's 1988 book *The Predicament of Culture* rejects an historical vision of the world as populated by endangered authenticities and 'makes space for specific paths through modernity'(5), expressing a 'utopian, persistent hope for the reinvention of difference' (15). Clifford believes that the privilege accorded to natural languages and 'natural cultures' as grounds for meaning and identity is dissolving. The development of electronic ways to process Japanese script, although a continuation of difference rather than a reinvention, does of course support the notion of Japan making its own specific path through the modern world rather than being absorbed into a wider global network of romanisation. This particular instance of a 'specific path through modernity', however, runs counter to the suggestion that language and culture no longer retain their significance as determinants of identity in a postmodern world. By successfully developing this technology which has allowed kanji to be used on the Internet, Japan has succeeded in keeping its subjectivity firmly anchored in culture and language, in particular in the script which is arguably the most concrete and widely visible manifestation of the culture and language to other eyes. We find here, therefore, none of the disjunction between culture and locale we have seen predicted by Waters in a globalised world. In the case of Japanese script, geographical location remains very much a predictor of social practice and preference. The orthographic boundaries, however porous they may become, remain unchanged.

This continued use of characters with computers, in particular on the Internet, has led to criticism from some quarters; the one area where romanisation continues to be sporadically advocated as a desirable option has been that of computer-mediated communication. Yamada, as we have seen in various contexts throughout this book, has consistently argued (eg 1994) that the use of characters prevents completely satisfactory communication between computers at international level, despite the adoption of the Unicode and other systems, and Hannas (1997) criticises the performance gap in terms of speed, applications, storage, retrieval and input between computers using alphanumeric systems and those using characters. While it is certainly true that using characters on computers does entail more work than the alphabet in a variety of ways, Japanese users are happy to continue the practice, as we can see from the continued rapid growth in availability and sales of Japanese-language applications. Hannas' argument, though forcefully and imaginatively expressed, makes no mention at all of the infrastructure considerations of a move towards romanisation in a highly industrialised, highly literate society such as Japan. The implications for education and the publishing industries in particular constitute the single most important reason why this will not happen, especially when combined with the affective or emotional resistance to any such change.

The use of kanji on the Internet therefore cannot be realistically described as an instance of language nationalism, underlining the maintaining of separateness and autonomy of script in any premeditated way. The concept of language nationalism, taken to its logical conclusion, usually implies an element of deliberate choice or agency, often coupled with an element of exclusion of those outside the nation at the same time it seeks to include or unite those within it. It would be difficult to argue convincingly for any such overt decision-making on the part of communications policy makers in Japan; no evidence for any such mindset exists, even in the records of deliberations of the National Language Council. The use of characters on the Internet does not seek to exclude – information is made freely available, but on the terms of the giver, as is the case with other languages. Kanji on the Internet are simply proof of a new technology having overcome previous problems and allowed the existing infrastructure to continue unchallenged. And the so-called linguistic 'bamboo curtain' is now crumbling as increasing numbers of non-Japanese worldwide demonstrate both a willingness to engage with the task of learning the script and a facility in doing so.

A comment from a paper presented at a 1993 conference on the history of science in East Asia sums up neatly the issues which the development of electronic character processing involve for Japan's international profile:

> Facing the coming global, information-oriented society in the 21st century, the world is now in a period of transition. There are two trends to note: one is the trend to make information sharable and commonly useable world widely; the other is, on the contrary, to actively create differences, especially to maintain the differences between cultures, in order to produce new information. The point is to keep these trends well balanced, and language will always play the central role in this. (Yokoi 1993: 4)

In orthographic terms, then, this technology has enabled the sharing of information on a much wider scale than before through the Internet while at the same time maintaining script-symbolised cultural differences and resisting romanisation. One of the most interesting language-related developments which the next century will bring will be the playing out of the endgame of this trend: will the kanji barrier fall as Japanese becomes more and more an international language and/or as its presence on the Internet increases? Or will the perpetuation of characters continue to wall off information in a linguistic ghetto, as Yamada gloomily prognosticates? Or will there, unlikely as it now seems, be a total about-face and adoption of romanisation after all, as some argue must inevitably eventually occur? The possibilities are intriguing and the outcome, at this transitional stage of Japan's change from hard to soft culture, difficult to forecast.

Notes

1 This is the Unicode/ISO-10646 Unified 'Ideographs' CJK Code, a character encoding standard comprising 20,902 characters which was settled in 1992. It is a unified 16-bit encoding scheme which allows systems to exchange information unambiguously. The CJK Joint Research Group is compiling lists of additional characters. This information was found, and more is available, at the following Web sites:
http: //jupiter.aist-nara.ac.jp/~yuuki-h/iso2022/jp/Unicode-Ideographs.html (part of Notes on CJK Character Codes and Encodings)
http: //www.ua.ac.be/KB/pn/pnoerr0.html#contents (Dr Peter L.Noerr, Character Sets and Unicode)

2 The Realtime Operation Nucleus, a project begun in 1984 aimed at developing a computer 'anyone can use as easily as driving a car', using a Japanese operating system.

References

Abe, K. (1995). 'Nihon ni oyonda "pasukon gannen" keieitai nimo eikyōryoku', in *Asahi Nenkan 1995*, Tokyo: Asahi Nenkan, 290.

Amano, S. (1991). 'Moji no honrai no yakuwari wa nani ka', *Shinika* 2 (10): 66–67.

Andō, S. (1988). 'Waapuro no fukyū to kokugo kyōiku: doko ga mondai ka?', *Kokugo Kyōiku Kenkyū Nenkan* (1988): 100–103.

Aoyama, Y. (1991). *Kaden*, Tokyo: Nihon Keizai Hyōronsha.

Atsuji, T. (1991). *Chiteki Seisan no Bunkashi: Wapuro ga motarasu Sekai*, Tokyo: Maruzen.

Befu, H. (1983). 'Internationalization of Japan and nihon bunkaron', in Mannari, H. and Befu, H. (eds) *The Challenge of Japan's Internationalization: Organization and Culture*, Nishinomiya: Kwansei Gakuin University and Kodansha International, 232–266.

Brown, R. A. (1986). 'Orthography in contemporary Japan: reality and illusion', unpublished Ph.D. thesis, University of Texas at Austin.

Buell, F. (1994). *National Culture and the New Global System*, Baltimore and London: John Hopkins University Press.

Campbell, C. (1992). 'The desire for the new: its nature and social location as presented in theories of fashion and modern consumerism', in Silverstone, R. and Hirsch, E. (eds) *Consuming Technologies: Media and Information in Domestic Spaces*, London: Routledge, 48–64.

Campbell, C. (1995). 'The sociology of consumption', in Miller, D. (ed.) *Acknowledging Consumption: a review of new studies*, London: Routledge, 96–126.

Clarke, J. (1918). *Japan at First Hand*, New York: Dodd, Mead and Company.

Clifford, J. (1988). *The Predicament of Culture: Twentieth-Century Ethnography, Literature, and Art*, Cambridge, Mass. and London: Harvard University Press.

Dale, P. (1986). *The Myth of Japanese Uniqueness*, London and Sydney: Croom Helm.

Economic Planning Agency (Business Statistics Research Division, Research Bureau). (April 1997). *Current Consumption Survey*. Statistics gathered from http: //jin.jcic.or.jp/stat/stats

EMarketer. (17/3/1999). "Is the Web finally becoming multilingual?", http: //www.emarketer.com/estats/031599_multi.html

EMarketer. (30/6/1998).
http: //www.emarketer.com/estats/net_geography_exp.html

Endō, O., Kuwabara, F., et al. (1987). 'Waapuro jisho o tensaku suru', *Kotoba* (8): 63-127.

Fujisaki, H. (1984). 'Wadopurosessa wa nihongo ni ihen o motarasu ka', *Kokubungaku (kaishaku to kyōiku no kenkyū)* 29 (6): 111-115.

Fujitsu Research Institute. (1998). http: //www.fujitsu.co.jp

Fukaya, T. (1984). 'Watashi no waapuro taiken', *Nihongogaku* 3 (7): 68-69.

Furukawa, H. (1962). 'Nihongo no moji insatsu no genjō to shōrai e no mitōshi', *Kokugo Kokuji* 10: 11-19.

Furukawa, S. (1991). 'Kanji busoku ni dō taishō suru ka? johōyō kanji shiron', *Shinika* 2 (4): 88-92.

Global Internet Statistics (by Language). (1998). http: //www.euromktg.com/globstats/index.html

Global Strategies. (1998). *Japanese Internet Statistics*, http: // www.globalstrategies.com/library/jdemo.html

Gottlieb, N. (1995). *Kanji Politics: Language Policy and Japanese Script*, London: Kegan Paul.

Hagiwara, K., Nakamura, S., et al. (1988). 'Kana kanji henkan no chiteki boken: waapuro kaihatsu wa kaku okonawareta', *Gekkan Nihongo* 1 (4): 10-17.

Hamaguchi, E. (1986). 'Kōdō jōhō shakai ni okeru "ningen" no mondai', in Hamaguchi, E. (ed.) *Kōdō Jōhō Shakai to Nihon no Yukue*, Tokyo: Nihon Hōsō.

Hannas, W.C. (1997). *Asia's Orthographic Dilemma*, Honolulu: University of Hawai'i Press.

Horii, R. (1990). 'Wapuro to tegami', *Nihongogaku* 9 (8): 60-65.

Iida, T. (1982) 'Ishiki, shuhō ni nani ga okorihajimeta ka'. *Asahi Jaanaru* 2/7/1982: 14-18.

International Telecommunications Union. (1997). Cited in 'Emerging market indicators', *The Economist* 8/8/1998: 88

Ishida, T. (1979). 'Nihongo waadopurosessa ni kitai suru', *Kana no hikari* (683): 9-14.
Ishida, T. (1982). 'Nihongo waadopurosessa o tsukatte kangaeru koto', *Kana no Hikari* (723): 5-15.
Ishiwata, T. (1988). 'Jōhō kiki no hattatsu to kokugo', *Bunkachō Geppō* (243): 16-18.
Itō, S. (1983). 'Waadopurosessa no shōrai', *Kokubungaku Kaishaku to Kyōzai no Kenkyū* 28 (11): 59-65.
Jackson, P. and Thrift, N. (1995). 'Geographies of consumption', in Miller, D. (ed.) *Acknowledging Consumption: a review of new studies*, London: Routledge, 204-237.
Japan Biztech. (1998). http: //www.nikkeibp.co.jp/MA
Japan Foundation Nihongo Kokusai Sentaa. (1995). *Survey Report on Japanese-Language Education Abroad 1993*, Tokyo: Japan Foundation Nihongo Kokusai Sentaa.
Japan MarkeTracker. (all dates 1998 and 1999). http: //www.internetjapan.com (searchable database).
Japan Statistical Association (ed.) (1992). *Japan Statistical Yearbook No. 42, 1992*, Tokyo: Statistics Bureau, Management and Coordination Office.
Japan Statistical Association (ed.) (1995). *Japan Statistical Yearbook, 1995*, Tokyo: Statistics Bureau, Management and Coordination Office.
Kabashima, T. (1982). 'Waadopurosessa o tsukau Pt 1', *Gengo* 11 (2): 84-89.
Kabashima, T. (1988). 'Wapuro wa nihongo o kaeru ka', *Nihongogaku* (7): 22-29.
Kabashima, T. (1989). 'Wapuro to kotoba', *Kokugo Kyōshitsu* (38): 7.
Kabashima, T. (1991). 'JIS kanji no igi to hyōka', *Gengo* 20 (3): 24-30.
Kabashima, T., Ichikawa, M., et al. (eds) (1987). *Konpyūtaa o Riyō suru Shō Chū Kōkō no Kokugo Gakushū*, Tokyo: Sankō Shobō.
Kaji, T. (1982). 'Insatsu to ofuisu ōtomeeshon', *Insatsu Zasshi* 65 (6): 84-86.
Kanda, Y. (1984). 'Nihongo o te de shaberu kikai', *Asahi Jaanaru* 4/5/1984: 85-88.
Katō, J. (1985). "Wapuro to kanji nōryoku', *Kyōikū Kenkyu* (1005): 84-86.
Kawada, T. and Amano, S. (1980). 'Nihongo no waadopuroseshingu', *Jōhō Shori* (August): 894-901.
Keizai Kikakuchō (ed.) (1990). *Heisei Ninenhan Kokumin Seikatsu Hakusho*, Tokyo: Ōkurashō Insatsukyoku.
Kida, J. (1991). 'Bunkateki hen'yō o ninau waapuro', *Shinika* 2 (4): 52-53.

Kida, J., Furuse, Y., et al. (eds) (1987). *Wapuro Kōgengaku*, Tokyo: Nihon Sofuto Banku Shuppan Jigyōbu.

King, F. (ed.) (1984). *Lafcadio Hearn: Writings from Japan*, Middlesex, England: Penguin.

Kitahara, M. and Aoki, R. (1982). *Konpyūtaa Gyōkai*, Tokyo: Kyōikusha.

Kodama, F. (1991). *Analyzing Japanese High Technologies: The Techno-Paradigm Shift*, London and New York: Pinter Publishers.

Kokugo Shingikai. (1992). *Gendai no Kokugo o meguru Shomondai ni tsuite: Shingi Keika Hōkoku*, Tokyo: Bunkachō.

Kokugo Shingikai. (1993). *Gendai no Kokugo o meguru Shomondai ni tsuite*, Tokyo: Bunkachō.

Kokugo Shingikai. (1995). 'Atarashii jidai ni ōjita kokugo seisaku ni tsuite: dai 20ki Kokugo Shingikai shingi keika hōkoku', in Kokuritsu Kokūgo Kenkyujo (eds) *Kokugo Nenkan 1995*, Tokyo: Shūei Shuppan, 427–453.

Kumon, S. (1986). 'Dentō bunka to nyū media', in Hamaguchi, E. (ed.) *Kōdo Jōhō Shakai to Nihon no Yukue*, Tokyo: Nihon Hōsō Shuppan Kyōkai, 62–69.

Kyanon Hanbai. (1988). *Sarariiman no Waapuro Katsuyō ni kansuru Chōsa*, Tokyo.

Lee, M. J. (1993). *Consumer Culture Reborn: the Cultural Politics of Consumption*, London: Routledge.

Lunde, K. (1993). *Understanding Japanese Information Processing*, Sebastopol, California: O'Reilly and Associates.

Maher, J. and Macdonald, G. (eds) (1995). *Diversity in Japanese Culture and Language*, London and New York: Kegan Paul International.

Maher, J. and Yashiro, K. (eds) (1995). *Multilingual Japan*, Avon, England: Multilingual Matters Ltd.

Manabe, K., Befu, H., et al. (1989). 'An empirical investigation of Nihonjinron: the degree of exposure of Japanese to Nihonjinron propositions and the functions these propositions serve', *Kwansei Gakuin University Annual Studies* (38): 35–62.

McGregor, R. (1995). 'Japanese paradox', *The Australian* 27/5/95

Microsoft Japan. (1998). http: //www.microsoft.com/japan

Miles, I., Cawson, A., Haddon, L. (1992). 'The shape of things to consume'. In R.Silverstone and E.Hirsch (eds), *Consuming Technologies: Media and Information in Domestic Spaces*, London and New York: Routledge, 67–81.

Miller, R. A. (ed.) (1969). *Bernard Bloch on Japanese*, New Haven and London: Yale University Press.

Miller, R.A. (1980). *The Japanese Language*. Tokyo: Tuttle

Miller, R. A. (1982). *Japan's Modern Myth*, New York: Weatherhill.

Miura, S. (1984). 'Waapuro wa pen ni kawatta', *Nihongogaku* 3 (7): 70-71.

Miyabara, M., Takeuchi, Y., et al. (1968). 'Hōritsuka to kanataipu (1)', *Shosai no Mado* (168): 18-26.

Miyoshi, M. (1989). 'Against the native grain: the Japanese novel and the 'postmodern' west', in Miyoshi, M. and Harootunian, H. D. (eds) *Postmodernism and Japan*, Durham and London: Duke University Press, 143-168.

Mizoe, M. (1982). 'Mō enpitsu o tsukau ki ga shinaku natta', *Asahi Jaanaru* 2/7/1982: 11.

Mizutani, S. (1982). 'Nihongo no shōraizō ni fuan wa nokoru ga', *Asahi Jaanaru* 2/7/1982: 23-24.

Mori, K. (1980). 'Nihongo no waadopurosessa: kana kanji henkan insatsu gijutsu', *Onsei Gakkai Kaihō* (165): 8-10.

Mori, K., Yamane, H., et al. (1988). 'Wapuro de nani ga kawatta ka', *Nihongogaku* 7 (12): 5-41.

Morioka, K. (1984). 'Watashi no waapuro taiken', *Nihongogaku* 3 (7): 72-75.

Moritani, M. (1982). *Japanese Technology: Getting the Best for the Least*, Tokyo: Simul Press.

Morris-Suzuki, T. (1988). *Beyond Computopia: Information, Automation and Democracy in Japan*, London: Kegan Paul International.

Mouer, R. and Sugimoto, Y. (1983). 'Internationalization as an ideology in Japanese society', in Mannari, H. and Befu, H. (eds) *The challenge of Japan's internationalization: organization and culture*, Nishinomiya: Kwansei Gakuin University and Kodansha International, 267-297.

Mouer, R. and Sugimoto, Y. (eds) (1989). *Constructs for Understanding Japan*, London and New York: Kegan Paul International.

Muramatsu, S. (1985). 'Wapuro no fukyū wa rōmaji undō ni kōki', *Rōmazi Sekai* (588): 52.

Murata, T. (1958). 'Kanataipu no genjō to mitōshi', *Gengo Seikatsu* (82): 18-25.

Murata, T. (1996). 'Intaanetto jidai no kanji', *Bungei Shunjū* 10: 90-92.

Nagao, M. (1980). 'Nihongo shori tekunorojii no genjō to shōrai', *Gengo Seikatsu* (350): 26-33.

Nagata, Y. (1989). 'Gendai nihongo ni okeru kanji no mondai', *Hyōgen Kenkyū* 50 (September): 66-74.

Najita, T. (1989). 'On culture and technology in postmodern Japan', in Miyoshi, M. and Harootunian, H. D. (eds) *Postmodernism and Japan*, Durham and London: Duke University Press, 3-20.

Nakajima, A. (1993). 'Konpyūtaa wa ningen no bunka o konpon kara kaetsutsu aru', in *Nihon no Ronten '94*, Tokyo: Bungei Shunjū, 666-667.

Nanbu, Y. (1996). '"Temps" are here to stay', *Look Japan* 478: 16-17.

Network Wizards. (7/1998). http: //www.nw.com

Nihon Jōhō Shori Kaihatsu Kyōkai. (1981). *Nihongo Waadopurosessa ni kansuru Chōsa Hōkokusho*, Tokyo.

Nikkei Multimedia. (1998). *Seventh Survey of Internet Active Users*, http: //www.nikkeibp.asiabiztech.com/Database/1999_Jan/13/Mor.04.gwif.html

Nishimura, H. (1986). 'Fakushimiri, zerokkusu, wapuro', *Bunkachō Geppō* (212): 10-11.

No author given. (1996). 'The Japanese word processor: creating a space where we want to play awhile', *The East* 6: 25-26.

No author given. (1991). 'Ofuisu kara kiete iku enpitsu', *Asahi Shinbun* 5/7/1991.

Nomura, M. (1984). 'Bunshō insatsuki kara bunshō sakusei no tame no waapuro', *Honyaku no Sekai* 9 (3): 16-19.

Nomura, M. (1986). 'Wapuro wa kokugo mondai o kaiketsu suru ka', *Gengo* 15 (7): 66-71.

Nomura, M. (1991). 'Jōhōka jidai no kanji to seishohō', *Gengo* 20 (3): 30-35.

NUA Internet Surveys. (1998). *How Many Online?* http: //www.nua.ie/surveys/how_many_online/asia.html

NUA Internet Surveys. (all dates). http: //www.nua.ie/surveys (searchable database)

Office of the Prime Minister (ed.) (1995). *Japan Statistical Yearbook 1995*, Tokyo: Bureau of Statistics, Office of the Prime Minister.

Ogata, Z. (1988). 'Kana-taipuraitaa to rōmazi-taipuraitaa no tōkeitekina hikaku kenkyū', *Rōmazi Sekai* (594): 20-23.

Ogi, M. (1984). 'Watashi no waapuro taiken', *Nihongogaku* 3 (7): 56-59.

Ogino, T. (1987). 'Kana kanji henkan shisutemu no nōryoku no shirabekata: VJE beta o rei ni shite', *Keiryō Kokugogaku* 16 (2): 81-87.

Ogino, T. (1987). 'Wapuro no fukyū wa nani o motarasu', *Kagaku Asahi* April 1987: 31-35.

Ogino, T. (1990). 'Wapuro jidai no nihongo', *Shinbun Kenkyū* (467): 20-23.

Ogino, T. (1992). 'Jōhōka to gengo kōdō hen'yō', in *Dai Ni Gun: Kōdo Jōhōka Shakai ni okeru Ningen Kōdō no Henka: Seika Hōkokushū*, Tokyo: Jūten Ryōiki Kenkyū 'Jōhōka Shakai to Ningen' Dainigun Jimukyoku, 28-42.

Ogino, T. (1994). 'Jōhōka to gengo hen'yō', *Nihongogaku* 10 (4): 63-70.

Ogino, T. (1994). 'Waapuro to gengo seikatsu', *Gendai no Esupuri* (319): 102-114.

Ōiwa, H. (1988). 'Wapuro nyūryoku wa kore de yoi no ka?', *Gengo* 17 (1): 48-49.

Passin, H. (1983). 'Overview: the internationalization of Japan - some reflections', in Mannari, H. and Befu, H. (eds) *The challenge of Japan's internationalization: organization and culture*, Nishinomiya: Kwansei Gakuin University and Kodansha International, 15-30.

Reed, S. (1993). *Making Common Sense of Japan*, Pittsburgh and London: University of Pittsburgh.

Robertson, R. (1992). *Globalization: Social Theory and Global Culture*, London: Sage Publications.

Rudofsky, B. (1974). *The Kimono Mind*, Tokyo: Tuttle.

Saeki, Y. (1987). 'Waapuro bunka ni okeru "kaku" to iu koto no imi', *Gekkan Kokugo Kyōiku* 7 (8): 56-61.

Saitō, K. (1989). 'Taipuraitaa arekore 1-6', *Rōmazi Sekai* (595): 14-39.

Saitō, K. (1989). 'Taipuraitaa arekore 7-12', *Rōmazi Sekai* (596): 18-42.

Sakai, T. (1983). 'Nihongo tōkikai shori', *Kyōiku to Jōhō* 308, 2-9.

Sakamoto, M. (1984). 'Watashi no waapuro taiken', *Nihongogaku* 3 (7): 62-65.

Sakamura, K. (1998). 'Japanese-language processing as conceived in the TRON Project'. Found at http: //tronweb.super-nova.co.jp/ jpnlangpro.html

Satake, H. (1983) 'Wapuro no fukyū to nihongo', *Kyōiku to Jōhō* (308): 30-35.

Satake, H. (1991). 'Waapuro to hojo kanji', *Gengo* 20 (3): 50-51.

Seeley, C. (1991). *A History of Writing in Japan*, Leiden: Brill.

Shimizu, T. (1988). 'Wapuro ni shinwa nashi', *Gekkan Nihongo* 1 (4): 18-19.

Silverstone, R. and Hirsch, E. (1992). 'Introduction', in Silverstone, R. and Hirsch, E. (eds) *Consuming Technologies: Media and Information in Domestic Spaces*, London: Routledge, 1-11.

Silverstone, R., Hirsch, E., et al. (1992). 'Information and communication technologies and the moral economy of the household', in Silverstone, R. and Hirsch, E. (eds) *Consuming Technologies: Media and Information in Domestic Spaces*, London: Routledge, 15-31.

Sōgō Kenkyū Kaihatsu Kikō (1983). *Erekutoronikusu no Shakaiteki Inpakuto ni kansuru Kenkyū*, Tokyo: Sōgō Kenkyū Kaihatsu Kikō.

Strathern, M. (1992) 'The mirror of technology', in Silverstone, R. and Hirsch, E. (eds) *Consuming Technologies: Media and Information in Domestic Spaces*, London: Routledge, vii-xiii.

Sugimoto, Y. (1996). 'Post-industrial Japan with post-modernity,' in M.Low and H.Marriott (Eds), *Japanese Science, Technology and Economic Growth Down-Under*, Monash Asia Institute: Clayton, Melbourne, 1996, 142-157.

Suzuki, Y. (1984). 'Ofisu ōtomeeshon no genjō', *Kyōiku to Jōhō* (317): 18-30.

Takahashi, A. (1983). 'Kokuji kaikaku to waadopurosessa', *Kana no Hikari* (736): 5-8.

Tanaka, A. (1991). 'Gendai hyōki ni hitsuyōna kanjisū', *Gengo* 20 (3): 59-61.

Tanaka, A., Tawara, M., et al. (1992). 'Gendai no kokugo o megutte', *Monbu Jihō* (1382): 8-17.

Tanaka, R. (1991). *Wapuro ga Shakai o Kaeru*, Tokyo: Chūō Kōron.

Tatsuoka, H. (1984). 'Moji kikai to moji seikatsu', *Kana no Hikari* (739): 3-10.

Terai, S. (1988). 'Ishikawa-kenka no kigyō ni okeru nihongo waadopurosessa no riyō jōkyō to ishiki no chōsa', *Kanazawa Joshi Tanki Daigaku Kiyō* (30): 151-164.

Tezuka, A. (1984). 'Nihongo waapuro o tsukatte mite', *Nihongogaku* 3 (7): 66-67.

Toyama, K. (1994). 'Different strokes', *Look Japan* November 1994: 39.

Toyota, S. (1988). 'Wapuro wa kanji no sukunai bunshō o', *Kana no Hikari* (795): 1104-5.

Toyota, S. (1989). 'Kanataipu to wapuro', *Kana no Hikari* (801): 513-515.

Tsukahara, Y. (1982). 'Waapuro sakubun kenkyūkai o tsukurō', *Kana no Hikari* (723): 21-22.

Tsunoda, T. (1985). *The Japanese Brain: Uniqueness and Universality*, Tokyo: Taishūkan Shoten.

Tsuruoka, T. (1991). 'Waapuro no shiyōzen to shiyōgo: shiyō moji no keiryōteki kenkyū', *Jōetsu Kyōiku Daigaku Kokugo Kenkyū* (5): 1-12.

Tsūsan Daijin Kanbō Chōsa Tōkeibu (ed.) (1987). *Shōwa 61nen Kikai Tōkei Nenpō*, Tokyo: Ōkurashō Insatsukyoku.

Tsūsan Daijin Kanbō Chōsa Tōkeibu (ed.) (1986). *Wagakuni Sangyō no Genjō*, Tokyo: Tsūsan Shiryō Chōsakai.

Tsuzugi, Y. (1984). 'Wapuro o tanoshinde mimasen ka', *Gekkan Shinjiyū Kurabu* 8 (85): 62-69.

Twine, N. (1991). *Language and the Modern State: The Reform of Written Japanese*, London: Routledge.

Uemae, J. (1975). 'Shōwa nijūichinen: kokugo shingikai', *Shokun!* 7 (7): 156-180.

Umesao, T. (1988). *Nihongo to Jimu Kakumei*, Tokyo: Kumon Shuppan.

Unger, J. M. (1987). *The Fifth Generation Fallacy: Why Japan is Betting its Future on Artificial Intelligence*, New York and Oxford: Oxford University Press.

Unger, J. M. (1996). *Literacy and Script Reform in Occupation Japan: Reading between the Lines*, New York and Oxford: Oxford University Press.

various (1989). 'Nihongo ga kawatta! waapuro no shutsugen de nihongo no bunshō wa dō henka shita ka', *Da Capo* (176): 21-2.

Wajcman, J. (1994). 'Technological a/genders: technology, culture and class'. In L.Green and R. Guinery (eds). *Framing Technology: Society, Choice and Change*, Sydney: Allen and Unwin, 3-14.

Waters, M. (1995). *Globalization*, London and New York: Routledge.

Wilkinson, E. (1991). *Japan versus the West: Image and Reality*, London: Penguin Books.

Yamada, H. (1984). 'Wapuro to nihongo no genjō to shōrai', *Nihongogaku* 3 (7): 4-17.

Yamada, H. (1989). 'Wapuro to kokuji mondai (1)', *Kana no Hikari* (806): 1003-1008.

Yamada, H. (1989). 'Wapuro to kokuji mondai (2)', *Kana no Hikari* (807): 1105-1108.

Yamada, H. (1994). 'Ōsugiru kanji/kango ni dō kotaeru ka', *Gakujutsu Jōhō Sentaa Kiyō* (6): 1-56.

Yamaneki, T. (1988). 'Waapuro tegami o kangaeru', *Mukōgawa Kokubun* (31): 90-97.

Yamasaki, S. (1982). 'Kana taipu wa jidai okure ka', *Kana no Hikari* (723).

Yamasaki, S. (1984). 'Kokugo undō toshite no kanamoji undō', *Kana no Hikari* (739): 12-14.

Yamashita, T. (1983). 'Waapuro jidai to kanamojikai', *Kana no Hikari* (736): 3-4.

Yokoi, T. (1993). 'Chinese characters, languages and computers', *Seventh International Conference on the History of Science in East Asia*, Kyoto.

Yokoyama, M. (1984). 'Hatokiin seketeshiu: kikai onchi wapuro o kiru', *Sakushin* (26): 63-79.

Yoshida, S. (1984). 'Kikai jisho ni tsuite', *Nihongogaku* 3 (7): 26-35.

Yoshino, K. (1992). *Cultural Nationalism in Contemporary Japan: A Sociological Enquiry*, London and New York: Routledge.

Yunomae, T. (1996). 'Commodified sex (sexism): Japan's pornographic culture', in AMPO (ed.) *Voices from the Japanese Women's Movement*, New York: M.E.Sharpe, 101–110.

Index